MARCO

P9-CQX-040

AUSTRALIA

with Local Tips

*The author's special recommendations are
highlighted in yellow throughout this guide*

There are five symbols to help you find your way around this guide:

★

Marco Polo's top recommendations – the best in each category

sites with a scenic view

⊙

places where the local people meet

🧍

places where young people get together

(148/A1)
*pages and coordinates for the Road Atlas of Australia
and the City Map of Sydney on page 38
(**O**) area not covered by maps*

*This travel guide was written by Klaus Viedebantt.
He lives with his Australian wife "down under" and has written
several books about Australia.*

MARCO ⊕ POLO

Travel guides and language guides in this series:

Alaska • Algarve • Amsterdam • Australia/Sydney • Bahamas • Barbados
Berlin • Brittany • California • Canada • Channel Islands • Costa
Brava/Barcelona • Costa del Sol/Granada • Côte d'Azur • Crete • Cuba
Cyprus • Dominican Republic • Eastern Canada • Eastern USA • Florence
Florida • Gran Canaria • Greek Islands/Aegean • Ibiza/Formentera • Ireland
Istanbul • Lanzarote • London • Madeira • Mallorca • Malta • Mexico • New York
New Zealand • Normandy • Paris • Prague • Rhodes • Rocky Mountains
Rome • San Francisco • Scotland • South Africa • Southwestern USA • Tenerife
Turkish Coast • Tuscany • USA: New England • USA: Southern States
Venice • Western Canada • Western USA

French • German • Italian • Spanish

*Marco Polo would be very interested to hear your
comments and suggestions. Please write to:*

North America:
Marco Polo North America
70 Bloor Street East
Oshawa, Ontario, Canada
(B) 905-436-2525

United Kingdom:
Geo Center International Ltd
The Viables Centre
Harrow Way
Basingstoke, Hants RG22 4BJ

*Our authors have done their research very carefully, but should any errors or omissions
have occurred, the publisher cannot be held responsible for any injury, damage
or inconvenience suffered due to incorrect information in this guide*

Cover photograph: Koala (Bilderberg/E. Grames)
*Photos: Author (4, 62, 67, 68, 70, 81, 92, 119); AV Aktiv (75, 89, 104, 115, 138, 142);
HB Verlag (113); R. Irek (9, 128); Lade: BAV (22, 116, 122), Sandhofer (100), Thompson (86, 96);
Mauritius: Fritz (12, 30, 77, 125, 131), Hubatka (155), Keyphotos International (16);
Kord (37, 46, 56), Krimminger (90), Matassa (19), Vidler (6, 34, 40, 72, 83, 107); Schuster: Ikeda (45);
Thomas (102); Transglobe: Boyer (26), Deichmann (54, 60), Fauner (110), Simmons (7)*

2nd revised edition 2000
© Mairs Geographischer Verlag, Ostfildern, Germany
Translator: Robert Levine
Editorial director: Ferdinand Ranft
Chief editor: Marion Zorn
Cartography for the Road Atlas: © Mairs Geographischer Verlag
Design and layout: Thienhaus/Wippermann
Printed in Germany

CONTENTS

Discover Australia!

A youthful culture on an old continent

Koala bears and kangaroos are without a doubt popular symbols of the fifth continent – although some Australians, taking a candid look at their fellow countrymen, would say that beer cans and barbecues would be more fitting. According to this rather critical view, most Australians would know the leaping marsupial or the cuddly eucalyptus eater that once served as a model for the teddybear only from their visit to a zoo because they have never been to the Australian wilderness known as the *Outback.*

It is interesting to note that this country, which so frequently and successfully advertises its largely untouched wilderness, is in fact one of the most urbanized in the world. More than 85 percent of the 19 million Australians live in cities, primarily in the metropolitan areas of Sydney and Melbourne. Adelaide, Brisbane and Perth have also developed into cities of more than a million inhabitants. For most Australians living in the cities, the *outback* has

become an everpresent myth comparable to that of the Wild West in North America. Many "Aussies" talk about the idea of setting out into the arid red heartland of their continent, but very few of them actually do. As a result, many Australians, tend to envy the foreign tourists who flock to their country in increasing numbers to explore the hot desertland in the interior.

Australia is not only the most arid continent in the world – next to Antarctica – but also the smallest at "only" 7.68 million square kilometers. On the other hand, since it is inhabited by a single nation only, it is also one of the world's largest countries: its surface area is roughly the same size as the continental United States of America without Alaska. Australia has no international boundaries on its land and is divided into six states and the Northern Territory which enjoys nearly the same rights as the states. Arranged in order of size, they include Western Australia, Queensland, Northern Territory, South Australia, New South Wales, Victoria and Tasmania. In addition, there are the Australian

Devil's Marbles – an apt name for these rocks on the Stuart Highway

Different countries, different hazards for motorists

Capital Territory around the federal capital Canberra and a number of island territories as well as a huge section of Antarctica. Australia is also the flattest continent, with only one major mountain range running along the east coast. The *Great Dividing Range,* which culminates in 2228 m high Mount Kosciuszko, is continued geographically in the mountains of Antarctica – a reminder that in the preshistoric past, Australia was, along with Africa, South America, India and Antarctica, part of the ancient southern continent of Gondwanaland.

From time immemorial, Australia has been isolated from the rest of the world, and that is why the fifth continent has devoloped a unique fauna and flora quite different from those found in the rest of the world. The kangaroo and the koala mentioned earlier are both part of a group of animals called marsupials with many different species. Marsupials have become almost extinct on other continents and also include the wallabies, a smaller relative of the kangaroos, the wombats and the ubiquitous opossums. There are also some species which have been in existence since primordial times, such as the duck-billed platypus, a type of mammal that lays eggs instead of bearing live young, and the saltwater crocodiles which can grow up to 7 m long and are also encountered in fresh water – extremely dangerous reptiles, which prey on both animals and human beings.

Also highly dangerous, although much less aggressive, are 70 of the 110 types of snakes which are found in the Australian bushland. To escape the scorching heat during the day, they like to withdraw into the shade of the eucalyptus or gum trees with their mighty light-coloured trunks and sparse foliage which are found in Australia in almost as many different varieties as the wattle trees, a kind of acacia. The warm yellow of their flowers and the dark green of the eucalyptus leaves have become the unofficial national state colours of Australia.

The polarity of the mythical *outback* and the sobering reality of everyday life has led to the development of a lifestyle which is clearly urban but far from metropolitan. The typical Australians live a rather unspectacular life somewhere in suburbia – a way of life that has come to be associated with such symbols as the barbecue grill in the garden and the rotating clothes rack in the backyard. In addition, since all of the major cities on the Australian continent are situated by or close to the sea, Australians have also developed a unique beach culture. The civilian heroes of Australia are the lifeguards who are identified by their swimming caps which are tied under the chin. When they hold their parades or competitions, the beaches are usually crowed with even more people than usual. Most of them are attracted by the glorious sunshine which rules most days of the year in Australia, but the price that the sun-worshippers pay is the highest rate of skin cancer in the world. The risk has increased dramatically with today's ozone-layer depletion in the southern hemisphere, and Australians are beginning to recognize the importance of protecting their skin against excessive exposure to the sun.

But suburbia also manifests the Australians' fundamental belief in a classless society. Most of the homes are very similar, each with a small garden, and everyone spends their leisure time in much the same way, drinking beer and barbecueing steaks amidst a relaxed discussion about sports or the much-loved horseracing bets. This apparent equality actually draws a misleading picture, however, for there are of course both affluent and grim neighbourhoods, and the current economic straits make it increasingly difficult for a young couple to purchase a home of their own. Still the myth of everyone being equal is carefully cultivated, and anyone who considers himself superior is sure to meet with the hostility of those around him. This deeply rooted idea clearly does not foster the creation of an élite, but on the other hand it does have its advantages when you visit the country. Being sincerely friendly-minded and helpful, most Aussies will treat foreigners (provided they are not Asian immigrants) as their equal and welcome tourists with open arms almost anywhere.

This notion of equality is as old as the history of white settlement on the *terra australis,* the southland, which dates back more than

Lifeguards on the Gold Coast

200 years. The modern history of Australia began with the establishment of a prison colony in the year 1788 when the British sent the first convicts to the recently discovered new land at the far end of the world. Although certainly not the first European to set foot on the new continent, James Cook had claimed the east coast of Australia for the British Crown in 1770. For a long time the fact that Australia began as a colony of convicts proved a major obstacle on the way to independence – in the minds of most Britons it simply continued to be a former penal colony. Today this disparaging view of Australia is no longer felt in Britain, but even so until well into the 20th century Australians saw themselves as an outpost of British civilization in the South Pacific and failed to develop an identity of their own. Change was brought about only by the two World Wars, when Australia was forced to loosen its ties with the increasingly powerless homeland and to look to the United States for protection. In fact, Australia has a lot in common with the U.S.A.: both countries came into existence at about the same time, both were hard won in the struggle against the forces of nature, and both systematically ignored the rights of the native population of the land – a fact that continues to be played down in both countries.

But there is one important difference: From the beginning, the United States has seen itself as a melting pot of nations, and this idea has always provided a strong impetus. Australia, however, has continued to think British until the recent past, and the pioneering achievements down under

were rarely recognized in the homeland and tended to be played down as tales from the backwoods. Until World War II, London was regarded as the measure of all things, as it were. To Australians, both of the world wars made one thing quite clear: Australia was a huge, rich continent which needed more people if it was to survive and to fend off the onslaught of the masses of people from the poor neighbouring countries in Asia. The greatest peril came when Japanese troops landed in New Guinea in 1942 and prepared to invade Australia.

Contrary to previous immigration policies, which had favoured the British and the Irish, Australia began to open its doors to southern Europeans after the end of World War II. The influx of Italians, Yugoslavs and Greeks led to fundamental changes in the traditionally British culture, and the British influence was pushed into the background more and more. The American way of life, which the American soldiers had brought to Australia, also began to make itself felt. In the minds of many Australians, it has actually come to replace British traditions today.

Nevertheless, the majority of immigrants are still British, and the Queen is still the official head of state of the *Commonwealth of Australia.* Next to Australian Football, a variation of rugby, cricket is still the most popular sport on the fifth continent. But apart from that, British traditions and attitudes no longer dominate the average Aussie's thinking. In fact, there is a now strong movement, led by the Labour Party, which is

8

pressing for a complete separation from the Crown.

In recent years Australians have begun to develop a more assertive and open-minded stance towards their Asian neighbours who had been largely ignored until the end of World War II – out of a sense of superiority as well as a genuine lack of interest. In addition, Australians still had unpleasant memories of the Chinese immigrants who had come to the fifth continent at the time of the goldrush in the mid-19th century and quickly acquired wealth and influence by working extremely hard.

The end of the Second World War brought dramatic changes to the South Pacific. When the UK joined the European Community, Australia's economy was forced to look for new markets. In the past, most of the agricultural products from down under, such as butter and cheese, lamb and wool had been exported to Great Britain. Now Australians turned to Asia, but the Australian farmers soon found that they could not sell their products in Asia unless they were prepared to open their own markets. But imports from low-cost countries such as Japan, Korea, Taiwan, Thailand or Singapore hit a raw nerve as the Australian economy turned out to be much less competitive than expected. The reasons for this were historical as well as economical: Australia was

Idyllic Coral Bay in Ningaloo Reef National Park, Exmouth

so rich in resources that it had never really cared about any competition: there are plentiful supplies of raw materials including gold, urainium, diamonds, rare precious metals, coal and natural gas. Oil is not quite so abundant, but there is enough to meet domestic needs. There are still vast treasures hidden in the red soil, and so Australians tended to feel that their *lucky country* could simply afford anything. To them, anything meant a rather lax work ethic and lots of leisure time. As a result, the much lower wages paid to workers in the neighbouring Asian countries obviously jeopardized Australian jobs. However, the Australian trade unions, always ready to go on strike, protected their members by forcing politicians to raise the duties on foreign imports. As a result of these protective barriers, the entrepreneurial spirit began to wane. Australia seemed happy to live off its reserves. When world market prices for raw materials fell, the agricultural exports still guaranteed a steady income, and vice versa. This carefree attitude prevailed until the 1980s when the world market prices for both agricultural products and raw materials hit a dramatic new low. This came as a hard-hitting shock to a population which had become used to a high standard of living and found itself suddenly faced with a rapid fall in the Australian dollar.

Since the early 1990s Australia has tried to balance its budget with a policy of austerity designed to make the economy more competitive on an international scale. At the same time, Australian foreign policy began to follow a more liberal course in an attempt to overcome the stagnation within the country. Asia had already become Australia's main partner in trade, but now the government in Canberra made an effort to establish itself as an important political player in the region. The economy has already shown signs of improvement. Industry has become much more innovative, and the trade unions have become increasingly reluctant to call for strikes – particularly in the wake of the painful experience with the month-long strike of airline pilots which badly crippled the economy. Foreign investors are still holding back,but prospects for the future are clearly encouraging.

The new orientation towards Asia, fostered by the USA, does seem to aggravate internal problems however. Many "Aussies" are still skeptical of this new Asian policy, particularly with regard to Japan – the war is still remembered. Japan is by far the largest market for Australian raw materials, and the Japanese car industry holds the lion's share in the Australian automobile market. In addition, the Japanese are playing an increasingly significant role in the tourist industry as both the number of Japanese visitors and Japanese investment are on the increase. Many of the resorts and hotels on the east coast are already owned by the Japanese, and that has caused some concern. It also shows, however, that tourism has become a major industry – as proven by the increasing numbers of visitors from all over the worlds who are coming to Australia and not just for the koalas and kangaroos.

History at a glance

c. 70,000–50,000 BC
Aborigines migrate to Australia from Indonesia

c. 12,000 BC
The rising sea level separates Australia from Indonesia and Tasmania becomes an island

A. D. 1606
Dutchman Willem Jansz sets foot on the north coast of "New Holland"

1616
Dutchman Dirck Hartog lands on the west coast

1642
Abel Tasman reaches Tasmania, naming it Van Diemen's Land

1770
James Cook claims Australia for the British Crown

1788
The first convicts arrive at what is now Sydney

1796
Commercial sheep-breeding begins with the first merinos

1806
William Bligh, sea-captain of the "Bounty" during the famous mutiny, is appointed governor of the penal colony

1813
The Blue Mountains are crossed for the first time and the interior is developed for agriculture

1851
The Gold Rush begins

1873
Ayers Rock is discovered

1901
The Australian colonies decide to form a Commonwealth

1915
Australian and New Zealand troops (Anzac) are butchered at Gallipoli in Turkey

1927
The Federal Government moves from Melbourne to Canberra

1932
Sydney Harbour Bridge is ceremoniously opened

1942
Japanese bombing raids on Darwin

1956
Olympic Summer Games are held in Melbourne

1972
Great Britain joins the European Community and Australia loses its principal market

1983
Australia wins the America's Cup, the world championship yacht race

1988
Bicentennial celebrations

1999
Sydney builds new stadiums for the Olympic Games 2000, some venues are already being used

From boomerangs to Waltzing Matilda

Culture, history, politics – a useful compendium for newcomers to Australia

Aborigines

They are thought to have come to Australia some 50,000 years ago across the land bridge from Indonesia which still existed at the time. When the sea level rose, these stone-age people lived in isolation on the new continent for centuries – until James Cook first set foot on Australian land. From that day on, the white man drove the Aborigines from their fertile lands, and alcohol and the white man's diseases brought from Europe have brought them dangerously close to extinction. Only through special legislation have the Aborigines and their unique culture survived. Their traditions centre around the concept of "dreamtime" – that magical realm of their ancestors in which the past, the present and the future are as one. The beliefs of the 500 or 600 different tribes of Aborigines are closely linked with nature, and for them, there are many unusual places which are regarded as sacred sites. Inevitably, this has brought conflict with the white man who is often interested only

Australian Aborigines

in exploiting the natural resources found in these places. There are close to 280,000 Aborigines living in Australia, many of them in special reserves. Even more than 200 years after the arrival of the first Europeans they seem to be unable to adapt to the white man's way of life. In recent years, however, more and more Australians have learned to appreciate the unique culture of the Aborigines.

Boomerangs

There are various types of boomerangs or "throwing sticks" which are used for different purposes – mostly for hunting, but also for ritual ceremonies. Not all of them are designed to return to the thrower. Hunting boomerangs, which are up to 1 m long and, properly thrown, can be used to kill even large kangaroos, are usually non-returning. Unlike spears, boomerangs are not used by all tribes of Aborigines. In most of the rural tourist centres in Australia, visitors can learn how to throw a boomerang. If you buy a boomerang in one of the souvenir shops, you will often be disappointed to find that it will not fly properly, much less return to your hand once you have thrown it – even if you have mastered the technique.

Bushrangers

In the early years of the Australian penal colonies, convicts frequently escaped into the as yet uncharted bush. Known as bushrangers, they often waylaid stagecoaches and other travellers, either single-handedly or in gangs. In later years, other criminals, who did not come from penal colonies, also went into the bush and soon formed gangs which also terrorized settlements and robbed banks and merchants. In those days, the majority of white Australians were either convicts or descendants of convicts, and they had little love or respect for the police authorities. That may help to explain why many bushrangers became folk heroes, and some of them have retained a special place in the hearts of Australians. The most famous of these bushrangers was a man named Ned Kelly, who was hanged in 1880 at the age of 26. He has since become a national legend and a cult figure. It is often said that many of the bushrangers only took from the rich and gave to the poor. Of course it is true that they took from the rich – it was not worth the trouble to try and rob the poor – but in most cases the pickings went into their own pockets.

Down under

The expression "down under" first coined by the British, indicated not only that the colony of Australia was on the far side of the globe; it also implied a certain amount of derision and disdain for the uncouth backwoodsmen who lived there – for the British clearly saw themselves as being on top of the world while Australia was at the bottom. In time, however, the term *down under* has lost this derogatory meaning and is now used as a rather affectionate way of referring to Australia (and sometimes New Zealand as well). Very few, if any, British people today entertain a condescending attitude towards their Australian cousins and many are keen to visit the country.

Immigration

Next to North America and New Zealand, Australia still ranks as one of the main countries open to immigrants from all over the world. In the past decade, however, the government in Canberra has imposed much more severe conditions for prospective immigrants. Apart from temporary immigration out of humanitarian considerations (for example with regard to the Vietnamese boat people) Australia now admits only those newcomers who are likely to benefit the country. This includes business people who have the financial means to create new jobs, and also professionals with skills which are in short supply in Australia. These professions, which currently include electronics engineers in particular, are compiled in a frequently updated list that is available from all Australian embassies and consulates. For information contact the visa section of your nearest Australian embassy.

Railways

Railway enthusiasts from all over the world come to Australia because the fifth continent offers a rare opportunity to cross from one side of the continent to the other by train and many other rail journeys. The most popular long-distance trains include the *Ghan* running between Adelaide, Melbourne or Sydney, and Alice Springs as well as the *Queenslander* operating between Brisbane and Cairns. A newcomer is the *Great South Pacific Express* between Sydney, Brisbane and Cairns for nostalgic luxury travel.

Film industry

The Australian film industry actually began before the Hollywood studios even opened. A documentary film was made by pioneering film producers in 1896, and the Australian Salvation Army commissioned a feature film three years later. Up to the invention of "talkies" the Australians were able to keep up with the Americans, but then a widening market required higher costs than the Australians could afford. The long tradition was, however, revived during the 1970s. Films such as *Picnic at Hanging Rock* won world-wide acclaim. Directors such as Peter Weir have become sought after by Hollywood. Australian films like *Mad Max, Crocodile Dundee* and *Shine* have been box office successes all around the world, and today Australia can once again boast a busy and internationally respected film industry.

Flying Doctors

The *Royal Flying Doctor Service* is a highly efficient medical organization which has no equal anywhere else in the world. In order to provide medical services for the Aborigines and the remote farmhouses in the vast outback, the Flying Doctors have established 13 base stations all across Australia. They are linked by radio with their patients, some of whom are thousands of kilometres away. For minor ailments, the doctors prescribe medication over the airwaves. Standard medical supplies are stored in all farmsteads in identical, carefully labelled medicine cabinets. In the event of a serious illness, however, the doctors will fly to their patients and transport them in their specially-equipped aircraft to the nearest hospital. The service was founded in 1928 with the aid of the *Australian Inland Mission.* The Flying Doctors have also become the stars of a TV series aired world-wide. Their bases are open to visitors.

Football

Australia's most popular sport is Australian Rules Football. Cities such as Sydney, Perth and Brisbane have spent huge amounts of money building up teams to challenge the supremacy of Melbourne, but the most successful teams continue to come from Hawthorn, Essendon and other suburbs of Victoria's capital. "Footy" as it is generally called, is a combination of rugby, old Irish ballgames and European football (soccer). It is one of the toughest and fastest team games played anywhere in the world. During the football season, which is in the Australian winter, this popular sport attracts tens of thousands of spectators. The Grand Final is always held in Melbourne and over 100,000 fans usually turn out for this great spectacle.

Posing for a tourist photograph: five cuddly koalas in a row

Women

The stereotype image of Australia as a macho society, while justified well into the 1960s, is becoming less and less true. The nation's early history as a penal colony, and its relatively one-sided population structure, created a society in which women, at least in public, played only a minor role. The achievements of many of the early female pioneers made little difference, nor did the electoral emancipation of women. Australia actually gave women the right to vote in 1902, a year after the country won independence, and was one of the first countries to do so. But in practice, in the business world and in politics, women remained at a disadvantage. The wave of immigration from southern Europe and later from Asia turned the clock back even

further. Today, however, women are occupying more and more management positions, both in business and in politics. The bastions of Australia's macho world are slowly toppling.

Casinos

In the puritanical atmosphere of post-war Australia, gambling casinos were frowned upon and banned. That is until 1973, when the conservative Federal State of Tasmania, of all places, permitted the opening of a casino in Hobart, the island's state capital. For many years, Tasmania profited from its special status, but eventually other states recognized that here was a source of income worth millions of dollars. Objections on moral grounds were abandoned, as the state treasurers saw their financial situation benefiting. Even

Victoria has a casino now, with Melbourne boasting the biggest in the country. Visitors can play roulette, baccarat etc. Two Up, a game that started in pubs, has become the unofficial national game, played with two coins, which are tossed in the air after bets have been placed on the possible combinations of heads and tails.

Art, music and the theatre

In Australian society's early years, there was little money to spare for such luxuries as the fine arts. There were more important things to do. It wasn't until 1943 that the government finally founded the *Arts Council of Australia,* a body charged with the mission of sponsoring the arts. Art forms that were not merely replicas of European ideas had appeared earlier. The first independent style of painting was produced by the artists who in 1880 made up the Heidelberg School, a group of painters who named themselves after a suburb of Melbourne. Around 1940, Russell Drysdale, a painter of international renown, provided the impetus for many new currents and ideas; developments that were not repeated until 1960 with the arrival on the scene of Sydney Nolan. In the meantime, Aboriginal art followed its ancient traditions and developed independently, although Albert Namatjira, who was successful in the European artistic arena, was an exception. In recent times, young Australian artists have turned increasingly to Aboriginal forms of expression for their inspiration.

Other art forms followed a similar pattern of development.

Ballet, for example, was introduced to Australia around 1940 by European immigrants. Since then, Australian ballet companies have achieved worldwide recognition.

The theatre was, of course, the first of the performing arts to find a captive audience among the prospectors in the gold towns in the middle of the last century. However, no real progress was made until 1950 when state-funded organizations such as the *Australian Elizabethan Theatre Trust* appeared. Jack Hibberd is among the most famous of Australian playwrights. Music, too, needed state funding and the establishment of the *Australian Broadcasting Company (ABC)* in 1932, before it could flourish. The ABC supports six of the country's eight symphony orchestras. Opera was, surprisingly, an early starter, not least because of the reputation of Nellie Melba, an Australian singer and one of the great names of 19th century opera. Rather predictably, the finest years of her career were spent abroad. It was 1956 before the *Australian Opera Company* gave its first performance. Sydney's finest building, the Opera House, opened in 1973, now stages many world-class productions. Joan Sutherland, one of the most famous divas of our century, who ended her stage career in 1991, is also from Australia.

Literature

Literature was the first art form to really flourish in Australia, thanks mainly to the *Bulletin* (now the country's leading news magazine), which, from about 1890, began to promote writers who took up Australian themes. Henry Lawson and Andrew "Banjo" Peterson, who wrote poems and short stories about life in the bush, quickly gained a following and are still widely read today. Bush ballads continue to be an important element of native Australian literature. Many other novel writers, including the Nobel Prize winner Patrick White, turned to the Australian landscape and the people who live there for their subject matter. Others drew on the years that they spent abroad, focussing on issues of international importance. Among the best known of these are Thomas Keneally, Morris West and Colleen McCullough. It was the latter who earned worldwide success with her novel *The Thorn Birds.*

National Parks

Australia's first national park, which is not far from Sydney, was opened way back in 1879. Most of the other national parks, however, were not established until the middle of this century. It was only in 1975 that the federal government in Canberra set up the *Australian National Parks and Wildlife Service (217 Northbourne Av., Turner, ACT 2601).* This body has been given the responsibility for administering a number of national parks around Ayers Rock and the Kakadu National Park in the far north. Most of these reserves have specially-marked campsites and other types of accommodation, but not all of them are open all the year round. In most cases, the parks are the responsibility of

the state they are in. All the addresses are available from the *Australian Tourist Commission.*

National Trust

Following the model of many other English-speaking countries, each of the Australian states has a National Trust whose responsibility it is to preserve for posterity the countryside, buildings, and other sites of special beauty or historical importance. With their own resources, these organizations have been able to purchase some 200 buildings and parcels of land and, where necessary, restore them. All the properties are open to the public, but an admission fee is payable. For information, contact the *National Trust of Australia, 71 Constitution Avenue, Canberra ACT 2600.*

Outback

For Australians, the Outback is not just a geographical term, but also a part of their consciousness. This inhospitable, hot, dry terrain, which extends deep into the interior of the continent, has no fixed boundaries and covers about three-quarters of the country. It is not easy to distinguish between the Outback and the bush, the steppe-like stretch of wilderness between the inhabited areas and the desert. All Australians declare that at some time in their life they will take a trip into the Outback, but for most of the inhabitants of this highly urbanized nation such an expedition remains an unfulfilled dream. They are certainly missing something. It is a unique experience to set off into this

"Road Trains" are huge trucks with trailers, up to 50 meters long, which speed across the continent on the dry, dusty roads

seemingly lifeless, but nevertheless impressive wasteland, where rain rarely falls and the sun beats down relentlessly. To go in search of barely visible traces of Aboriginal settlements and sacred sites in the company of an expert guide, and then to return in the evening to the billy-can hanging over the campfire is as typical an experience of Australia as admiring the Sydney Opera House or exploring the Great Barrier Reef. The Outback is still an untamed region, even if it is crossed by a network of unmade tracks for the "road trains", huge lorries with up to three trailers, in which two or three tiers of cattle or sheep are transported. If you see one of these monsters of the road approaching, it is worth pulling off the track for a minute or two.

Horses

There are many nations in the world which are obsessed with horses, but perhaps none more so than gambling-crazy Australia. Where else does a horse-race give rise to an offical holidays? Where else could a horse be the cause of an international incident, as was the case of Phar Lap, the most successful horse in Australian history? The horse's death in mysterious circumstances at an American race meeting gave rise to top-level diplomatic exchanges. The legendary horse has since been stuffed and is on display in Melbourne's National Museum.

Melbourne is also the venue for the country's biggest horse race. The Melbourne Cup is held on the first Tuesday in November at the Flemington racecourse. This occasion has all the grandeur of Ascot, together with the popular appeal of a colourful carnival. Cup Day is a public holiday in the Melbourne metropolitan area. This two-mile race, which was first run in 1865, brings the whole of Australia to a standstill for three minutes. If you are in Melbourne in November, it is an event that should not be missed.

Horse-racing has a long tradition in Australia; it is said that the first race was held in 1799. When the first fleet arrived in Botany Bay in 1788 with their cargo of convicts, there were also seven horses on board. Five of them escaped into the countryside. These were the ancestors of the wild horses or "brumbies" which roam around the interior in herds.

Politics

The Commonwealth of Australia, to give the country its correct name, has a political structure similar to that of Great Britain. The head of state is the Queen, who is represented in Australia by a governor-general. There is, however, pressure for change. It is felt that the links with London are inappropriate for a proud, independent nation.

The Australian parliament consists of two bodies: the House of Representatives and the Senate. Representatives are elected every three years. Senators every six years. The largest party forms the government and chooses the Prime Minister. In practice, Australia has a two-party system, although the conservative camp is made up of the Liberal Party and the National Party. At the other end of the spectrum is the Australian Labour Party, a party which has predominantly social democratic leanings. The most significant of the smaller parties is the Australian Democrats.

Foreign policy has changed quite dramatically in recent years. Up until the 1980s the country looked towards Europe and the USA for its markets, but the politicians have now recognized that Australia is part of the Pacific Rim and that business must look to its Asian neighbours if it is to survive. In internal politics, each state has its own constitution and can exercise considerable influence with the national government. Although turn-out is high for elections due to compulsory voting, generally speaking Australians tend to express little interest in politics.

School of the Air

The children who live on isolated farms in the Outback are clearly unable to travel hundreds of kilometers every day to the nearest school. Instead, they receive their education by radio, via the School of the Air. At certain prearranged times, all the children on a farmstead will gather around the radio and receive their lessons from their teachers at school headquarters.

From time to time, children fly out to regional centres for short spells of residential classes or examinations. Older children requiring further education must attend a boarding school. The School of the Air is an offshoot of the Flying Doctor Service and its radio network. The first radio-linked school opened in Alice Springs in 1951 and, like the Flying Doctor Service, the school headquarters is also open to visitors.

Sports

Between the 1950s and the 1970s Australia was one of the world's top sporting nations. Australian swimmers, tennis players and athletes dominated their sports. The pinnacle of their achievements was the 1956 Olympic Games staged in Melbourne. The team, dressed in their traditional green and yellow jerseys, won 35 medals, including 12 gold medals. Today, despite a number of superb individual performances, Australia no longer rates highly among the world's big name in sport. Sydney, however, is the proud host of the 2000 Olympic Games.

The most popular of all spectator sports down under is what is called "Australian Rules" Football, although cricket also regularly commands large crowds of spectators and the Australian national cricket team is one of the leading sides.

One of the greatest achievements in Australia's sporting history occurred in 1983, when a sailing team sponsored by the millionaire Alan Bond, whose business empire collapsed in the early 1990s, managed to wrest the America's Cup from the New York Yacht Club. Four years later, the ornate trophy was recaptured by an American crew after a race in Australian home waters off Fremantle.

Stockmen

Americans call them cowboys; Australians call them stockmen. They patrol the land on horseback, checking the cattle in the vast pastures, although helicopters, piloted by specialists, are now also a part of modern livestock control. Many of the stockmen are Aborigines, who are considered to be particularly skillful riders and herdsmen. These heroic farm-hands even have a museum dedicated to their trade, the *Stockman's Hall of Fame (Landsborough Highway, Longreach 4730 Qld.)*.

Waltzing Matilda

While *God Save the Queen* is played on all royal occasions, the official national anthem is *Advance Australia Fair*, although it has to be said that few people are familiar with the words. The same is certainly not true of *Waltzing Matilda*. Written in 1895 by Andrew "Banjo" Paterson, the song tells the moving story of how a hungry itinerant worker, who steals a lamb, is pursued and finally drowns in a billabong – a pond in a dried-up river bed. It should be noted that Matilda is not in fact the name of a woman, but a bundle containing the worldly possessions of a man "on the road". No one really knows who wrote the music. Some attribute the tune to Christina McPherson, others say that Paterson put new words to an old march. When Australians get together in large numbers, it's never long before a group somewhere breaks into a rousing chorus of Watzing Matilda.

Barbies, yabbies and pavlovas

Australia's cuisine offers untold culinary delights

Food

For many years, old-fashioned British cooking traditions continued to dominate the culinary scene on the fifth continent: Bland, unseasoned dishes served with boiled vegetables, salads without dressing, and a general absence of imagination in gastronomic matters were typical of Australian food. Mealtimes were a monotonous routine of steak "n" egg, roast lamb and meat pies with tomato sauce. Many of these hearty traditional dishes are still very popular with Australians, but aside from the fact that they can indeed be a veritable delicacy (but unfortunately seldom are), the general standard of home and restaurant cooking in Australia has come a long way in the last 20 years or so. Not only have the immigrants from southern Europe and Asia contributed exciting new culinary ideas – an increasing number of young

Australia offers a greater range of culinary delights than you might expect – a highly popular speciality being fresh seafood

and talented chefs have taken the traditional European approach and developed it by adding fresh local products. In the major cities, you can now find some excellent top-class restaurants, and the general quality of the middle range restaurants has also improved enormously. In all these places, kangaroo meat, low in cholesterol, is becoming increasingly popular.

The island continent offers its guests excellent fish and seafood dishes. Prawns, lobsters, mussels and oysters are all reasonably priced and well prepared in appetizing ways. Sydney rock oysters are widely recognized as being among the best in the world. "Yabbies", Australian freshwater prawns, are another speciality. The firm white flesh of the large barramundi fish (found mainly in Queensland and in the Northern Territory) is an Australian speciality, as is the delectable John Dory. Australia is one of the world's largest exporters of lamb and beef, both of which can be enjoyed at their best in their country of origin. Those who love fruit will also feel quite at home in Australia. Most of the fruits familiar to European and North American gardeners are grown in the cooler parts of southern Australia (Tasmania is renowned for its apples), while tropical fruits thrive in the hotter climate of the north. A famous Australian speciality (admittedly New Zealand also has claims with respect to its origins) is the fruit pavlova. It consists of meringue, whipped cream and fresh fruit. This delicious – if extremely rich in calories – dessert was named in honour of Anna Pavlova, a well-known Russian ballet dancer.

One of the country's most famous culinary institutions is the "barbie". Nearly every garden has its own barbecue corner with a grill on which meat, sausages or prawns are cooked. In all the national parks and in most of the destinations favoured by holiday-makers and day-trippers, you will find gas-fired grills where, for a few cents, anyone can prepare his own barbecue in a matter of minutes. And of course no Aussie picnic basket is complete without a bottle of tomato sauce. To foreigners, this Australian national sauce may taste just like the familiar American ketchup, but Australians swear that there is a world of difference. One undisputed Australian speciality is Vegemite, a blend of plant extracts, which looks like sump oil and smells of yeast – similar to the British spread, Marmite. Australians love this spread, and it is guaranteed to be found on practically every breakfast table, even in international hotels. Aussies prefer their Vegemite on sliced cheese especially, while foreign-ers usually give it wide berth. Even New Zealanders, who share many preferences with their Australian neighbours, shun Vegemite in favour of the British Marmite, a similar spread made from yeast extract – although most visitors generally see and taste absolutely no difference between the two.

Beverages

Australians follow closely behind the Bavarians and the Belgians as the largest per capita consumers of beer, although the trend seems to have reversed in recent years. Brands such as Foster's in its characteristic blue can, VB (short for Victoria Bitter) in green, or XXXX (called Four X) in yellow, are widely exported to other countries as well. Beer is always served ice cold. In many pubs, it is drunk straight from the bottle or can. In the summer, the cans are kept cool in polystyrene chiller boxes. These boxes, often with the name of a pub printed on the side, make good souvenirs, as do the T-shirts and tea towels also printed with a pub logo. In many pubs, you can order a jug of beer for a whole table. Whenever someone is buying a round, remember that it is customary always to reciprocate in kind. For a long time, men have found it socially unacceptable to drink wine in public, but this attitude is also beginning to change. Wine bars are now being established especially in the cities, and even in the pubs it is now possible for a man to order a glass of wine without inviting funny looks. After all, Australia today produces world-class wines. The best known of the 600 or so wineries are situated near Adelaide, Melbourne, Sydney and Perth. The principal wine producing regions are the Barossa Valley in South Australia and the Hunter Valley in New South Wales. As in the vineyards of Europe, it is possible to taste the local wines in the wineries. A small sample is usually free. If you order a glass, you may have to pay for it, but, if you then decide to buy a few bottles, this charge is usually deducted from your bill. In most wine regions, organised tours to several different vineyards are available. These tours are thoroughly recommended, not least in view of the fact that there are strict alcohol limits for those driving on Australia's roads, and the police rigidly enforce this regulation with frequent alcohol tests.

Restaurants

In all Australian states you will find both licensed and unlicensed restaurants. The latter are usually referred to as BYO (Bring Your Own). All of these restaurants invite their guests to bring their own wine, beer or any other alcoholic beverage. The barman will provide the glasses and also put your bottles or cans in the refrigerator and open them for you on request. He will also provide ice cubes and soft drinks for mixers. In most cases, the restaurant will charge a small corkage fee for this service, usually about A$ 1 per person. Wine connoisseurs in particular appreciate this arrangement, as they can not only save money – they can also enjoy their favourite vintage along with their meal. As alcohol licenses are expensive, many restaurant owners opt for a BYO in order to offer their customers more affordable dishes. Specialist shops, known as bottle shops, stay open until late in the evening to cater for BYO restaurant customers. They also sell chilled drinks.

As in the UK, many pubs also serve counter meals. These light dishes are ordered and collected at the bar. Fast food outlets, which sell anything from hamburgers to Asian food, are as popular in Australia as they are in Europe. British-style fish and chip shops also abound, but here you will find a striking difference. Instead of cod and plaice, you can enjoy barramundi, red emperor, John Dory and flake (shark) which are freshly fried and served with the chips. For price and quality, a fish and chip shop is a wonderful alternative with great food at hard-to-beat prices. A typically Australian institution is the milk bar. Unlike in the past, however, it is often little more than a counter in a shop selling sweets, food and newspapers etc. Milk shakes are still very popular drinks in Australia, but as the fruit flavouring is nearly always artificial these days, they are often rather disappointing. Thick shakes are milk shakes with one or two scoops of vanilla ice-cream mixed in. Smoothies are another type of milk shake which have ice-cream and chunks of fresh fruit added. In recent years, many milk bars have been replaced by cafés serving espresso and cappucino, giving rise to an Italian-style coffee-house culture.

Pink diamonds and fiery opals

The finest souvenirs from Australia
are elegant and expensive, but sports gear is a good alternative
– and often one season ahead

As a Western style country with a thriving economy and a strong youth culture, the range of goods available in Australia is not vastly different from anywhere else in Western Europe or North America. The often-voiced charge that Australian shops are behind the times and sell the fashions that were all the rage the previous year in London is no longer justified. On the contrary, in the world of sports especially, young Australian designers are now producing innovative clothing for both men and women. Sportswear and leisure clothing as worn in Australian cities are still considered a close secret as the majority of the young Australian designers have not yet gained international recognition.

More recently, the "Outback look" has become fashionable. Long waxed coats and jackets by a company called "Driza-bone" (a word-play on *dry as a bone*) are definitely worth investing in if

A veritable shoppers' paradise:
Sydney's Queen Victoria Building

you are looking for weatherproof clothing. They are good quality and really do resist even a rainstorm. When you are wearing one of these coats, you may look like someone straight out of a "spaghetti western" – particularly if you complete your outfit with a wide-brimmed "Akubra" hat, as popularized throughout the world by Crocodile Dundee. Remember, however, that these particular hats and coats are not cheap. There are also less expensive imitations around, but they are not of the same quality.

In a country where sheep have played such an important role in shaping the history and economy, sheepskin products are very good value, though they are difficult to take home when you have airline luggage restrictions to contend with, but worth considering if you have any spare space in your suitcase. Sheepskin coats, boots, gloves, hats and rugs are widely available in a variety of different styles. However, you will also find some excellent, yet affordable, woollen products. In recent years, the colourful Coogi design pullovers and knitted jackets in particular have become increasingly popular.

Probably the most popular souvenirs of Australia, but also the most expensive, are the rare pink diamonds from the Argyle Mine in the north – and opals. Australia is the biggest producer world-wide of these shimmering semi-precious stones. In practically all the main tourist regions there are companies which have specialised in the sale of the national gemstone. Opals are relatively expensive, because there is no simple way of finding them in the ground, not even in the main centres such as Coober Pedy or Lighting Ridge. The most valuable stones are the rare dark opals, whose layers of colour on a dark background show a particularly colourful lustre; the majority of opals have a light-coloured milky background, however. This is why many Australian jeweller shops sell so-called triplets which consist of a thin layer of opal glued onto a dark, glass-like background and enveloped in a third transparent layer of glass for protection. Less expensive but also quite beautiful are the striped or dotted "zebra stones" from the northern parts of Western Australia. Natural pearls, which are usually sold in the form of jewellery, also come from this region. In the past, the search for mother-of-pearl was another important industry; these opalescent shells are still prized today and often used for jewellery. Occasionally souvenir shops will offer jewellery made from greenish-blue mother-of-pearl as typically Australian, but in most cases these so-called paua shells ac-

tually come from New Zealand or one of the smaller South Sea islands.

Works of art produced by Australian Aborigines make special souvenirs. The best places to look for them are the specialised galleries found in almost all major cities, but there are also special shops run by some of the Aboriginal cooperatives which sell the products made by their people. Aboriginal artists use the same forms and colours as their ancestors in their pictures, carvings, ornamental weapons and tools. Basically, one can easily differentiate between the styles of the native inhabitants from the arid interior and those from the hot and wet region on the north coast. The pictures and motifs created by artists from the "red heart" of the continent are almost exlusively composed of multicoloured dots and a few occasional lines. By contrast, the Aborigines from the north prefer the so-called "X-ray style" which is also found in some of the old cave paintings. In this style, human beings as well as animals are rendered in such a way that their bones and internal organs are visible. In the north, the Aborigines often paint on pieces of tree bark which of course are not available in the almost treeless interior. Many souvenir shops also sell "Aboriginal art" – more often than not this art is hastily produced and of no artistic value. The same is true for most of the boomerangs which are also found in these shops – some of them are even "Made in Hongkong". It can nevertheless be worthwhile to look around one of the typical souvenir shops, for among all the junk produced especially for gullible tourists you may also find some of those amusing and often kitschy trinkets which reflect the patriotric feelings of many Australians, such as an ice cube mould in the shape of the Ausstralian continent. Another good source for souvenirs and curio items are the flea markets. Information on dates and location can be found in the local newspapers.

Book collectors in particular should not miss the opportunity to look around in the antiquarian and second-hand bookshops in the cities. The huge stacks of used paperbacks may not be of much interest, but you will usually find some remarkable Australiana as well as shelves with interesting (and often inexpensive) works in German, French, Italian and other foreign languages. This has to do with the fact that Australia is a country of immigrants, and in many cases the children or grandchildren no longer speak and read their family's original language, so that many of the books from the family library are sold off when the older generation is no longer around.

A typical and quite delicious souvenir from Australia are macadamia nuts, although they are not exactly cheap. If you have ever been to Hawaii, you will probably know these nuts as a speciality of the islands, but actually the macadamia trees are native to Australia. It is true, however, that the Hawaiians have shown the Australians how such gifts of nature can be marketed with great success. This is obviously out of the question for another souvenir which is even more typical for the land down under: Vegemite. This unique sandwich spread, introduced in the preceding chapter on "Food & Drink," is sold in small jars especially for travelling. Such a glass of Vegemite is inexpensive and a great novelty for your next party at home. Airport shops and a number of stores in the larger cities now sell meat which has been specially packaged for export. In most cases, it will be filet mignon of beef which is sold at prices especially attractive for Japanese tourists in view of the beef prices in their home country. But increasingly you can also find kangaroo meat which would also make a great souvenir.

Most stores in Australia are open Monday to Friday from 9 am to 5.30 pm and on Saturday until midday. More and more shops are now open on Sundays as well. In the major cities, many stores stay open until 8.30 or 9 pm in the evening on a special "late shopping night" usually on Thursday or Friday. Food stores and newsagents (which also sell sweets etc.) frequently keep longer hours and also open on Sundays, at least on Sunday morning. When paying for the more expensive items, major credit cards or traveller's cheques (preferably made out in Australian dollars) are accepted in most stores. Banks in the main cities will also change foreign currencies, but you often need to show your passport. Commission rates can vary greatly. Some of the banks are already prepared to deal with the new "Euro" currency. Banks are usually open from 9.30 am to 4 pm on weekdays, and in most cases they will extend their hours during the "late shopping nights" mentioned earlier.

Celebrating a day at the races

Colourful parades and spectacular sporting events dominate the national celebrations

Australia is not a very religious country, and it is not surprising that very few church festivals are observed as public holidays. By way of compensation, there are many other festivities and events, athletic and otherwise. Many of them are set to take place in a certain month, but the exact date may vary from one year to the next. For details, you should turn to the local tourist offices. As an alternative, the Australian tourist Commission in your home country will also be glad to help by sending you a printed calendar with a complete list of major festivities and celebrations.

PUBLIC HOLIDAYS

1 January *New Year's Day*
26 January *Australia Day*
Good Friday
Easter Monday
25 April *Anzac Day* in commemoration of the heavy losses suffered by Australian troops during World War I

An exciting event: camel races at Alice Springs in the month of May

25 December *Christmas Day*
26 December *Boxing Day*
If any of these holidays should fall on a weekend, they are usually moved to the nearest Friday or Monday. (This custom is due to be changed, however.) In addition to these national holidays, each state also has its own public holidays. A good example is *Labour Day,* which is observed in all Australian states although on different dates.

FESTIVALS AND LOCAL EVENTS

January
Sydney to Hobart Yacht Race: The best-known and most exciting sailing competition in Australia begins on 29 December and ends on 2 January in the capital of Tasmania.

❖ *Riflemen's Festival:* A typical German-style beer and wine festival staged in Hahndorf (SA), originally a village of German settlers.

Australian Open: The first grand slam tennis tournament of the year in Melbourne (Wimbledon, Paris and New York follow).

❂ *Montsalvat Jazz Festival:* Australia's biggest jazz festival is held at the Montsalvat artists' colony in Eltham (Vic).

February
❂ *Kangaroo Island Racing Carnival:* The so-called *Picnic Races* in Kingscote on this island off the south coast of Australia are the highlight of a spectacular country fair.

Gay and Lesbian Mardi Gras: Colourful Shrovetide celebrations of the gay community, clothed and unclothed! With highly imaginative costumes, culminating in a gigantic parade before some 500,000 spectators in Sydney.

March
Adelaide Festival of Arts: Every other year (in even-numbered years only) the capital of South Australia hosts the most important arts festival in the country. The festivities last three weeks and feature international artists performing in a variety of concerts as well as opera, theatre and ballet events.

Grand Prix: The world's top formula one race drivers competing in Melbourne.

✻ *Port Fairy Folk Festival:* Thousands of mostly young people gather in the small harbour town of Port Fairy (Vic) for Australia's greatest folk music festival on the Labour Day weekend.

March/April
Sydney Festival of the Rocks: In the week before Easter, a festival and parade are held in "The Rocks", the oldest historic district of Sydney.

April
Anzac Day parades: War veterans celebrate by holding memorial parades in many towns throughout the country.

May
Camel Races: In the Northern Territory the somewhat cooler month of May is the season for horse races as well as various races with tamed camels. The best-known camel races are held in Alice Springs.

★ *Melrose Mountain Festival:* The historic town of Melrose (SA) in the Flinders Range recalls pioneering days with this popular festival.

June
★ *Darwin Beer Can Regatta:* The capital of the Northern Territory holds boat races for vessels built from empty beer cans – a perfect occasion for a huge party.

July
❂ *Willunga Almond Blossom Festival:* Willunga (SA) is the heart of the largest almond-growing area in Australia. During the last week of July, when the almond blossoms announce the arrival of spring, the town is crowded with thousands of visitors.

August
Sydney City of Surf: More than 20,000 competitors take part in Australia's biggest annual running event. It covers a distance of 14 kilometres and ends in the suburb of Bondi Beach.

Warana: Brisbane's biggest festival presents a colourful mix of theatre, music and dance. The high

MARCO POLO SELECTION: FESTIVALS

1 Melrose Mountain Festival
This rustic festival held in autumn is well-known and popular among South Australians but still a true insider tip for their fellow countrymen and especially for tourists (page 32)

2 Darwin Beer Can Regatta
This is anything but a dry event: While the race is on, everyone is laying the groundwork for next year's boats – by emptying thousands of beer cans (page 32)

3 Henley-on-Todd-Regatta
A boat race in the literal sense of the word and a 'bottomless' barrel of fun. If they are lucky, tourists may get a chance to actively participate in the race (page 33)

point of festivities is a parade through the streets of the city.

September
❖ *VFL Grand Final:* More than 100,000 spectators gather in the Melbourne stadium for the Cup Final of the Australian Rules Football league. "Footy" is a tough contact sport, a mixture of football and rugby, which originated in Victoria and is played by teams throughout the country.

Royal Shows: September is the month of the great regional agriculture fairs known as the Royal Shows. The major events are held in Perth (WA), Adelaide (SA) and Melbourne (Vic), followed in October by Hobart and Launceston (Tas).

October
Melbourne Fringe Festival: For three weeks the metropolis celebrates the creativity of poets, actors, dancers, comedians, painters and sculptors with numerous exhibitions, performances and readings. The festival is a counterpart to the "official" Melbourne Arts Festival which takes place during that same month.

★ *Henley-on-Todd-Regatta:* The Todd River in Alice Springs (NT) does not have water every year, and in October the riverbed is usually dry. This is when an unusual race, named after the traditional British Henley race, is held with bottomless boats and strong-legged crews.

November
❖ *Melbourne Cup Day:* The country's most important horse race is held on the first Tuesday in November in Melbourne – a carnival for the city, a state holiday for Victoria – time to party for the rest of the country.

December
The great summer holidays begin this month, preceded by British style Christmas parties, with colourful hats and lots of confetti, which take place throughout the country in private homes, restaurants and offices.

"The most beautiful port in the world"

A city prepares for the Olympic Games in the year 2000

Australia's oldest and biggest city (pop. 3.5 million) is considered one of the most beautiful in the world because of its geographical location with countless bays and inlets and a natural harbour. An abundance of sunshine, a fine and

Waterfront promenade at Darling Harbour

varied culinary tradition and miles of beaches all add to this impression. These assets, combined with an ecological awareness and its location on the shores of the South Sea give it the quality of an Olympic city of the year 2000. Sydney's harbour extends a full 20 km inland, but it is no more than 8 km from the Heads, the narrow gateway to the Pacific Ocean, to the

---

Hotel and restaurant prices

Hotels
Category 1: over A$ 175
    (approx. 100 US$)
Category 2: up to A$ 175
Category 3: up to A$ 85
    (approx. 50 US$)
Prices are for a double room
without breakfast. Singles are
almost the same price.

Restaurants
Category 1: over A$ 45
    (approx. 25 US$)
Category 2: up to A$ 45
Category 3: up to A$ 25
    (approx. 15 US$)
Prices are for a meal with
starter, main course and dessert;
beverages not included.

Abbreviations

Av.	Avenue	**ACT**	Australian Capital Territory
Cr.	Circus		
Dr.	Drive	**NSW**	New South Wales
Hwy.	Highway	**NT**	Nothern Territory
Rd.	Road	**Qld**	Queensland
Sq.	Square	**SA**	South Australia
St.	Street	**Tas**	Tasmania
Tce.	Terrace	**Vic**	Victoria
		WA	Western Australia

Circular Quay. It was Captain James Cook who first identified the entrance to the harbour and gave it its name which is still used today: Port Jackson. But Cook never landed here. It was in 1788 that the first settlers – convicts and their guards – went ashore under the command of Captain Arthur Phillip. In the early years, the young colony had to contend with food shortages again and again, and life was tough for the convicts and the soldiers. Things changed only when the first free settlers landed at Port Jackson in Sydney Cove towards the end of the eighteenth century. Today Sydney is the capital of the most densely populated state in Australia, New South Wales, and a principal centre of commerce and industry. As far as tourism is concerned, Sydney is the most important city: It is here that the majority of visitors first set foot on the fifth continent. (**167/D 5–6**)

VIEWS OF THE CITY

Seen from the top of the 325 m high ✻ *Sydney Tower* (**38/B–C 4**), *in the Centrepoint Shopping Centre between Pitt and Castlereagh St.,* the bustling harbour, the skyline of the city, the elegant suburbs, the Pacific coast and, further inland, the Blue Mountains form an impressive panorama. The tower is *open 9 am–10.30 pm daily, on Sat to 11.30 pm; for information call 02/92 31 10 00.* The viewing platform is at the 305 m level, above the two revolving restaurants (one of them self-service) and a coffee and cocktail bar. Or you may climb up 200 steps inside the south-east pylon of the *Harbour*

MARCO POLO SELECTION: SYDNEY

1 Powerhouse Museum
This excellent museum in the Darling Harbour district – considered the best in Australia – offers a free tour showing the highlights of the collection every day at 1.30 pm (page 39)

2 Hyde Park
Sydney people eat only snacks for lunch, but they have developed their own lunch-time culture. Go to Hyde Park at midday to enjoy the wonderful variety of snacks offered at the many different stands (page 42)

3 Marble Bar
The most beautiful bar in all of Australia, saved from demolition at its original location in the city, has become a highly popular meeting place – especially on Friday nights (page 44)

4 Hawkesbury River
When the postman arrives by boat in the morning, he sounds his horn twice, and the residents of the houseboats come to the jetty to collect their mail. This unusual mail service has become a popular tourist attraction (page 45)

The imposing skyline of Sydney is best seen from Darling Harbour

Bridge (**38/B1**) to another 👁 viewing platform. The pylon itself houses the small *Harbour Bridge Museum.* The bridge, formerly the main landmark of Sydney but now second after the Opera, spans the harbour in a huge arch 503 m long and 134 m high. The pylon is *open 10 am–5 pm daily,* with access from the footpath across the bridge. To get there, follow *Cumberland St. in The Rocks, Tel: 02/92 47 34 08.*

SIGHTS

Darling Harbour (38/A 4–5)

The once shabby docklands have been cleaned up at a cost of millions and turned into a leisure and tourism area with more than 200 shops and restaurants. The 🏃 North Pavilion at Harbourside Festival Marketplace has become a popular meeting place especially for young people. Darling Harbour is linked with the city by a *Monorail (round trip 12 min., departures approximately every 4 min.)* and *Pyrmond Bridge* (**38/A5**). This pedestrian bridge was built as the first electrically operated swing-bridge in the world. The *Sydney Aquarium* (**38/A 4–5**) on the city side of Darling Harbour features crocodiles, coral fish and, visible from a glazed passage, sharks, rays and other impressive sea dwellers *(9.30 am–9 pm daily, Tel: 02/ 92 62 23 00).* The *National Mari-*

time Museum (**38/A4–5**, *9.30 am–5 pm daily, Tel: 02/9552 7777*) documents the maritime history of the island continent. The ★ *Powerhouse Museum* (**38/A6**, *10 am–5 pm daily, Tel: 02/9217 01 11*), housed in an old power station, focuses on technology and science as well as on special aspects of human life such as childhood. In just a few years it has become the most frequently visited museum in the country. Free concerts are held in the museum courtyard during the summer months. It is recommended that you reserve at least three hours for your visit to the museum. Other attractions in Darling Harbour include a *Chinese Garden* (*9 am–5 pm daily*), the *SegaWorld high-tech theme park* and nightly screenings of films projected onto a "screen" of moving water (*Tel: 02/9211 23 11*).

Fort Denison (O)

This small island fortress in the harbour was originally a prison and later became part of the fortifications built to protect the city against a feared attack by the Russian tsarist navy. Hegarty's Ferries offer boat tours which depart *Tue–Sun at 10 am, 12.15 am and 2 pm* from *jetty no. 6 at Circular Quai.* Reservations are recommended on weekends (*Tel: 02/9555 98 44*). Sydney folk refer to the small island as *Pinchgut.* Also open to visitors is the second former prisoners' colony at *Goat Island* (*Tel: 02/9555 98 44*).

Harbour cruises

✍ As well as the commercial harbour cruises there are also a number of much more inexpensive ferries, such as the ones to the *Taronga Zoo* (Australian and Pacific fauna, plus a fine view of the city) or to the beachside suburb of *Manly* on the Pacific coast. Several shipping companies specialize in harbour cruises, some of which include coffee and cake or even a full evening meal. Recommended for their highly competent commentaries are the tours offered by *Captain Cook Cruises.* A replica of the "Bounty" originally built for a film set is available for dinner cruises around the harbour. You can also rent sailboats if you want to explore the area by yourself. The ferries and many of the cruises depart from the piers of Circular Quay.

Homebush Bay (O)

This is the site of the new Olympic stadium facilities – a swimming complex already exists.

National Aboriginal Cultural Centre (O)

This Cultural Centre is the result of a close cooperation between private investors and numerous Aboriginal communities all over the country. Although a commercial venture, it offers a good insight into the culture of the Aborigines. The main attraction is a cast of dancers which perform four times a day. The admission fee to the Centre (but not the tickets for the performances) is refunded to you when you make purchases. *1–25 Harbour St., Tel: 02/9283 74 77, 9 am–8 pm daily*

Opera House (38/C1)

This structure with its bold, gleaming white roof has long become a national symbol of Australia. Guided tours are available except during performances. The building was designed by

Danish architect Jörn Utzon and officially inaugurated by Queen Elizabeth II in 1973 after a dramatic controversy over spiraling construction costs. The architect left the country even before the topping-out ceremony, announcing that he would never again set foot on this continent. Current billings are advertised in the local newspapers. *Guided tours lasting about one hour are available 9 am– 4 pm daily; Tel: 02/92 50 71 11*

Royal Botanical Gardens (38/C 2–3)

This vast park, which begins at the Opera House, covers an area of 24 hectares *(open daily from 6.30 am to sunset).* As well as Australian plants and trees you will find here a wide variety of species imported from other parts of the world, some of which are grown in huge greenhouses. A special section of the garden focuses on plants native to the outback and their various uses by Aborigines. Guided tours are scheduled twice weekly *(for information call 02/92 31 81 11).*

Sydney Explorer Bus

The 35 km route takes you to many of the important sights in Sydney. *With a day ticket (9 am– 7 pm, A$ 20, family ticket A$ 60) you can get on and off at any of the 27 stops as often as you like.* Red buses run approximately every 20 minutes, and tickets are available from the driver. The blue *Bondi & Bay Explorer* offers similar tours down to famous Bondi Beach. Especially recommended is the *Sydney Pass* which also entitles you to use the Sydney Explorer as well as the entire public transport system including the ferries. You have a choice of passes for 3,5 or 7 days. The cost is A$ 70–110 for adults and A$ 200–315 for the entire family. *Information: Tel: 02/92 55 17 88*

"The Rocks" is considered the most charming part of Sydney

40

The Rocks (38/B 1–2)

The oldest and most charming part of the city has been rehabilitated. Boutiques, souvenir shops and restaurants have created a colourful, lively scene, although the district has lost some of its former appeal with the new focus on tourism-based commerce. *The Visitors Centre, 104 George St., is open Mon–Fri 8.30 am–4.30 pm and Sat–Sun 10 am–5 pm.* This is also the point of departure for the guided walking tours through the historic district which take place several times daily *(Tel: 02/ 92 55 17 88).* Purchasing a "Rock Ticket" (A$ 36) entitles you to free admission at the *Earth Exchange Mining Museum* or the *Museum of Contemporary Art (10 am–5 pm daily, 6 College St., Tel: 02/92 41 58 92),* a guided walking tour, a harbour cruise and a meal in a Bavarian-style *Bierkeller.*

Vaucluse House (O)

The stately home of William Charles Wentworth, the "father of the Australian constitution" in the elegant district of Vaucluse has been turned into a museum. *Tue–Sun 10 am–4.30 pm, Olola Av., Tel: 02/93 37 19 57*

MUSEUMS

Art Gallery of New South Wales (O)

The state collection of New South Wales focuses primarily on works by Australian painters but also includes a number of European and Asian artists. The museum regularly presents special exhibitions on different subjects. *Mon–Sat 10 am–5 pm, Sun midday–5 pm, Art Gallery Rd., Tel: 02/92 25 17 44*

Australian Museum (38/C 5)

One of the largest collections in the country on natural history with a special department devoted to the mining of mineral resources, Australia's most important and profitable industry. Don't miss the wonderful collection on the Aborigines. *10 am–5 pm daily, 6 College St., Tel: 02/93 20 60 00*

Hyde Park Barracks (38/C 4)

Architect Francis Greenway, who came to Australia as a convict, designed some of the early classical buildings in Sydney, including these barracks at Hyde Park (1819) which now house a museum showing the life of the early settlers. *10 am–5 pm daily, Macquarie St., Tel: 02/92 23 89 22*

Museum of Contemporary Art (38/B 2)

❖ The collection focuses on Australian and international works of 20th century art. The museum café offers a fine view of Circular Quay. *11 am–6 pm daily, guided tours at midday, 1 and 2 pm, George St./First Fleet Park, Tel: 02/92 52 40 33*

Museum of Sydney (38/C 3)

This museum in the first Government House is devoted to the history of the city and its people. *10 am–5 pm daily, Bridge/Phillip St., Tel: 02/92 51 59 88*

Sydney Jewish Museum (O)

This "Museum of Tolerance" illustrates the history of the Jews in Australia and the story of their emigration to the fifth continent. Exhibits include a replica of a local street dating back to the year 1840. *Mon–Thu 10 am–4 pm, Fri 10 am–2 pm, Sun 11 am–5 pm, 148*

In the spirit of Marco Polo

Marco Polo was the first true world traveller. He travelled with peaceful intentions forging links between the East and the West. His aim was to discover the world, and explore different cultures and environments without changing or disrupting them. He is an excellent role model for the travellers of today and the future. Wherever we travel we should show respect for other peoples and the natural world.

Darlinghurst Rd. in the suburb of Darlinghurst, Tel: 02/93 60 79 99

OPEN SPACES

★ *Hyde Park* (**38/C 4–6**) in the heart of the city has become a popular meeting place especially at lunchtime – mostly due to the fact that in the basements of the surrounding shopping centres you can buy a wide selection of delicious foods from all over the world, notably Asian, Italian, Arab and others. In the city centre, at *Martin Place* (**38/B-C4**), there is little in the way of green spaces, but in the summer the square is the setting for performances by musicians, actors and other entertainers. The small park between *Circular Quay* (**38/B-C2**) and *The Rocks* is also a popular place to meet in the lunch break.

BEACHES

Manly and Bondi Beach   (**O**)
These are Sydney's most popular beaches, easily accessible by ferry or bus respectively. In recent years, however, they have become somewhat discredited due to increasing rubbish piles and the lack of a sewage disposal system. *Bondi* especially had a bad press. *Manly,* situated north of the harbour entrance, now has an *Information Centre* for tourists

(Tel: 02/99 77 10 88). ☀ Bondi's former Victorian splendour has certainly seen better days, but the beach is still popular with young people. All in all, Sydney can boast more than 20 beaches, including half a dozen within the bay. The *surfing beaches on the Pacific* are situated on both sides of The Heads, the entrance to the harbour, and extend in the south to historic Botany Bay, where James Cook first landed, and some 30 km to the north. Some of the beaches, like *Reef Beach* near Manly, have become nudist beaches, others are preferred by the gay community (Lady Bay Beach in the harbour) or by surfers (Narrabeen on the north shore). Most beaches are protected by shark nets and are also patrolled by lifeguards. It is strongly recommended that you do not venture into the water if there are no lifeguards on duty.

RESTAURANTS

Bathers Pavilion   (**O**)
A wonderful airy restaurant on the beach in the Balmoral district with the now fashionable "new Australian cuisine" which uses mostly local herbs combined with a variety of Asian spices. *4 The Esplanade, Balmoral, Tel: 02/ 99 68 11 33, Category 2*

Doyle's (O)

⤜ A popular fish restaurant on the beach at Watsons Bay. Although catering to the tourist trade and not exactly cheap, Doyle's is recommended for a pleasant evening. The same goes for its other restaurant on Circular Quay. *11 Marine Parade, Tel: 02/93 37 20 07, Category 1–2*

No Name (O)

❖ Affordable Italian-style cooking in East Sydney. Very busy, hence not the place for a quiet, romantic evening. BYO (bring your own). You will probably have to wait some time before a table is available. Coffee bar in the basement. *81 Stanley St., Tel: 02/93 60 47 11, Category 3*

Phillip's Foote (38/B 2)

This lively pub in The Rocks has a barbecue grill in the courtyard where you can cook your own steaks or fish. *101 George St., Tel: 02/92 41 14 85, Category 3*

SHOPPING

The *Queen Victoria Building* (QVB) on George Street (**38/B 5**) is considered one of the finest shopping centres in the world. In honour of their Queen, the local people erected an impressive complex in Victorian-style architecture which first opened in 1898 as a fruit and vegetable market. Today the renovated structure houses some 200 shops and restaurants. A special tip: Anyone interested in Australian films will probably find what he is looking for in the shop of the Australian Television ABC. Not far away are two other ele-

gant but smaller shopping arcades: the *Imperial* and *Strand,* both opening onto Pitt Street (**38/B 4–5**), the main shopping street of Sydney, and both lined with fine retail shops. Also on this street is Grace Brothers, a famous department store. Just a block away is its greatest competitor, David Jones on Market Street (**38/B 4–5**). The largest shopping centre in the heart of the city is the Centrepoint complex (**38/B 6**) on Pitt Street.

The finest shopping street outside the city centre is Oxford Street (**38/C 6**) in the Paddington district. Here you can relax from your shopping tour in one of the many small cafés and bistros. Other attractive shopping areas are the modern buildings in Darling Harbour and the restored old town in The Rocks. Be warned, however, that most shops in these areas cater mainly to the needs of the tourist.

HOTELS

Backpacker hotels, B & B guest houses and universities (O)

Sydney has a number of rather basic backpacker hotels, most of them located in the entertainment district around *Kings Cross.* A bed in a dormitory-style room costs as little as A$ 15 per night. Bed & Breakfast facilities are offered by various organizations; the largest is *Bed & Breakfast Sydneyside, P.O. Box 555, Turramurra 2074, Tel: 02/94 49 44 33.* The colleges and universities also offer inexpensive accommodation in the student dormitories during the holidays, especially in the months of December and

January. For information call the universities directly. The *Australian Youth Hostel Association XHA* has an office at *Kent St. 422, Tel: 02/92 61 11 11.*

Criterion Hotel (38/B 5)
Basic accommodation with relatively few amenities but very good location in the city centre. *22 rooms, Pitt/Park St., Sydney 2000, Tel: 02/92 64 30 93, Fax: 92 83 24 60, Category 3*

Inter-Continental Sydney (38/C 2)
This modern-style luxury hotel once housed the treasury office of the former colony – hence the historic hotel lobby with its pleasant café. *540 rooms, 117 Macquarie St., Sydney 2000, Tel: 02/92 30 02 00, Fax: 92 40 12 40, Category 1*

Kent All Regent of Sydney (O)
A pleasant private hotel in a beautiful location away from the city centre. All 22 rooms have been equipped with private baths. *122 Victoria St., Potts Point, Sydney 2011, Tel: 02/93 57 76 06, Fax: 92 51 28 51, Category 1–2*

Regent of Sydney (38/B 2)
⌘ Luxury hotel with a fantastic view of the harbour, frequently rated as the best hotel in Australia. The rooms on the harbour side offer a great view of the Opera House. The in-house restaurant *Kables* has won numerous gastronomic awards. *596 rooms, 199 George St., Sydney 2000, Tel: 02/92 38 00 00, Fax: 92 51 28 51, Category 1*

Travellers Rest Hotel (O)
Lower mid-range hotel in good location between the city centre and Darling Harbour. *85 rooms,* *37 Ultimo Rd., in the Haymarket district, Tel: 02/92 81 55 55, Fax: 92 81 26 66, Category 2*

Sydney is a metropolis that offers every kind of entertainment, from more than a dozen theatres and numerous jazz clubs to fashionable discotheques and the redlight district at Kings Cross – not to mention the countless pubs. The ★ *Marble Bar* in the basement of the Hilton (**38/B 4**, *259 Pitt St., Tel: 02/92 66 06 10*) deserves special mention. This historic bar, which has been purchased by the hotel, has become a favourite nightspot for yuppies and ex-yuppies of both sexes.

The busiest nightlife areas – apart from the red-light district of *Kings Cross* (**O**) – are *Oxford Street* (**38/C 6**), *Victoria Street* (**O**) and *Glebe Point Road* (**O**). Oxford Street runs from the city centre the fashionable district of Paddington ("Paddo") and is lined with shops and cafés which stay open until well into the night. Victoria Street begins near Kings Cross and ends at Potts Point. Glebe Point Road cuts right through the university area in Glebe and has an interesting mix of shops and bistros.

The disco and club scene is forever changing, and clubs can lose, or gain, their "in" status almost overnight. *CBD* (**38/B 4**, *75 York St., Tel: 02/92 99 89 11*) has been named after the usual abbreviation for the central business district. ✠ *DCM* (**O**, *33 Oxford St., in Darlinghurst, Tel: 02/92 67 73 80*), is a venue for "rave" and also, but not exlusively, a popular meeting place of the gay scene. The

✝ *Metropolis* (**O**, *Mount/Walker St. in North Sydney, Tel: 02/ 99 54 35 99)* is a club frequented mostly by young people from North Shore. ✝ *The Q Bar* (**O**, *44 Oxford St., in the Darlinghurst district, Tel: 02/93 60 13 75)* attracts those who love their music at top volume. *The Fringe and the Unicorn Hotel* is primarily a pub which also plays the latest in music trends. Especially on weekends it is difficult to get in unless you are "blonde and leggy". Clubs rarely get into full swing before 9 pm and continue until 2 am or even later at weekends.

Those who prefer jazz to techno will be better off in the traditional *Basement* (**O**, *29 Reiby Place, Tel: 02/92 51 27 97)*. Musicians from America and Europe often perform in this popular jazz club on Circular Quay. If you want to hear some of the local talent you should try the *Strawberry Hills Hotel* (**O**, *435 Elizabeth St., in the Surry Hills district, Tel: 02/96 98 29 97)*.

INFORMATION

Sydney Visitor Centre (38/B 2)
106 George St., The Rocks, 9 am–6 pm daily, Tel: 02/92 55 17 88, Fax: 92 41 50 10

SURROUNDING AREA

Blue Mountains (166–167/C–D 6–5)
Seen from a distance, this mountain chain some 70 km west of the city actually does look blue in the mist created by its eucalyptus trees. The rock formation of the *Three Sisters,* the *Wentworth Falls* near the resort of *Katoomba* and the *limestone caves* at *Jenolan* are the main attractions. *For more detailed information call the Blue Mountains Tourist Information Centre (02/ 47 82 18 33)*

The Blue Mountains seen from afar

Hawkesbury River (167/D 5)
★ The valley of the Hawkesbury River lies to the north of Ku-Ring-Gai Chase National Park. The river is especially popular with houseboat owners. Visitors can rent cabin cruisers or houseboats. As an alternative, you can take a cruise on the mail boat and accompany the postman on his rounds. The boat departs every weekday at 9.30 am from the pier at Brooklyn with additional tours at 1.15 pm on Thursday and Friday.

Ku-Ring-Gai Chase National Park (167/D 5)
This national park is located some 25 km north of the city and boasts almost 100 km of coastline with countless bays. The *Kalkari Visitor Center on Ku-Ring-Gai Chase Road (watch for the exit on the Sydney-Newcastle motorway) is open 9 am–5 pm daily. Tel: 02/ 94 57 93 22, on weekends call: 02/ 94 57 93 10*

A water sports paradise

From subtropical beaches to the biggest living coral reef in the world

The Pacific Highway is part of Highway 1 which follows the full length of Australia's coastline. It is one of the most popular routes for those who set out to explore the Australian east coast by car. Cairns in northern Queensland is usually the final destination for travellers heading north from Sydney. This route, which is some 2700 km long, follows the narrow strip of land between the ocean and the mountains of the Great Dividing Range and takes the motorist into a subtropical and finally a tropical landscape. On one side of the road lie endless beaches baked by the hot sun, on the other are the mountains with their somewhat cooler climate. And far out at sea on the horizon, one can see the waves of the South Pacific breaking all along the 2000 km long Great Barrier Reef which serves as a protective wall for countless islands. Some of them have been turned into exclusive holiday

Surfers Paradise on the Gold Coast offers everything surfers and sailing enthusiasts dream of

playground reserved for the happy few, others have been developed as holiday resorts with large hotel complexes. And of course there are many isles in this turquoise sea which are inhabited only by great flocks of seabirds. By Australian standards, this stretch of coastline is densely populated, and there is no shortage of accommodation, petrol stations and shops. Apart from the beaches, there are few tourist sights. The places described here follow the route northward towards the equator.

HUNTER VALLEY

(**167/D5**) For Sydney people, the wine-growing valley of the Hunter River, some 180 km from the city, is still within easy reach and hence a popular destination for short weekend trips, even more so because there are two national parks – *Ku-Ring-Gai Chase* and *Brisbane Waters* – as well as a much-visited theme park nearby: *Old Sydney Town* near Gosford is a kind of Disneyland of Australian history, a reconstruction of Sydney as it was around 1800, with costumed settlers and soldiers re-enacting their daily lives. *Wed–Sun 10 am–4 pm, open daily during school holidays. Tel: 02/ 43 40 11 04*

The main town in the region of the Hunter Valley is *Newcastle* (**167/D 5**), the second-largest city (pop. 260,000) in New South Wales. Founded back in 1804 as a camp for particularly dangerous convicts, Newcastle rapidly developed into a busy commercial port following the discovery of coal in the region. Today the city is not just an important coal-mining town but also an industrial centre with a large steel-mill. Generally speaking, the valley of the Hunter River is characterized by two industries which might seem mutually contradicting: coal-mining and wine-growing. In spite of the mining activities the countryside is still very attractive. The main centre of the wine-growing region is *Cessnock* (**167/D 5**, pop. 18,000).

There are close to 30 vineyards in the area around Cessnock. The majority of them welcome visitors for wine tastings. Some proprietors also offer guided tours of their cellars and bottling facilities. There are vineyards which date back to the mid-19th century, and some of them are among the best-known in Australia.

In and around Cessnock you will find a variety of wine restaurants of all categories. Especially recommended is the bistro of the *Hunter Valley Wine Society* on *Wollombi Rd. in Cessnock (Tel: 02/49 90 66 99), Category 3,* which promotes and sells the different wines produced in the region. Top-ranking establishments (in terms of culinary standards and prices) are the *Hunter Resort*

MARCO POLO SELECTION: EAST COAST

1 Panoramic flights
The true dimensions of the Great Barrier Reef, one of the great wonders, are best appreciated from the air. Flights (helicopters or light aircraft) are offered all along the coast (page 60)

2 Marlin season
From September to December, fishermen come to Cairns for the great marlin hunt – and paint the town red almost every night (page 58)

3 Mud crabs
In the months without an "a" in the name Brisbane's restaurants serve the tasty mud crabs. Try Breakfast Creek Wharf for the best (page 55)

4 Dunk Island
Not exactly the cheapest but arguably the most beautiful island on the Great Barrier Reef. It's the setting for "Confessions of a Beachcomber", one of Australia's best-known novels (page 60)

(Hermitage Rd., Tel: 02/49 98 77 77), the *Casuarina Restaurant (Hermitage Rd., Tel: 02/49 98 78 88)* and *Roberts at Pepper Tree (Halls Rd., Tel: 02/49 98 73 30)*.

ACCOMMODATION

Many of the hotels and motels in the region raise their room prices at weekends by 40 to 100 percent. In view of the great demand you should make advance reservations at weekends, particularly for rooms in the higher price range. Some of the conveniently located accommodations in the wine region are:

Cessnock Motel
20 rooms, 13 Allandale Rd., Cessnock, NSW 2325, Tel: 02/49 90 26 99, Fax: 49 90 58 34, Category 3

Pepper's Hunter Valley Guest House
50 rooms, Ekerts Rd., Pokalbin, NSW 2320, Tel: 02/49 98 75 96, Fax: 49 98 77 39, Category 1

The Convent Guesthouse
Halls Rd., Pokalbin, NSW 2320, Tel: 02/49 98 77 64, Fax: 49 98 73 23, Category 1

INFORMATION

Hunter Valley Visitor Information
Turner Park, Cessnock, NSW 2325, Tel: 02/49 90 44 77, Fax: 49914518

NEW SOUTH WALES

(167/D-F 5-2) Although Sydney with its millions of people is not far away, you can still find many quiet beach communities on the coast between Newcastle and Tweed Heads near the boundary between New South Wales and Queensland. Many construction projects for new hotels and new apartment buildings in some of the better-known resorts such as Port Stephens, Port Macquarie, Coffs Harbour or Byron Bayand indicate, however, that this stretch of the coast is gradually becoming a major tourist area. Fortunately, this development is kept in check by the fact that there are several national parks either directly on the coast or in the immediate hinterland.

Port Stephens **(167/E 5)** is located on a huge natural harbour more than twice the size of Sydney harbour. The bay is so big that watersports enthusiasts have no trouble finding a quiet stretch of beach in spite of the many Australian holiday-makers flocking to this area. *Port Macquarie* **(167/E 4)**, founded in 1818 at the mouth of the Hastings River, claims the honour of having been the first holiday resort in all of Australia. It was only in recent years that this harbour town has enjoyed a small boom with steadily increasing numbers of holiday-makers. The *Sea Acres* reserve, one of the last surviving rainforests in Australia, and a koala refuge station are the main attractions of the "Port", as the locals call their town. *Coffs Harbour* **(167/E 3)**, which tries to draw visitors with the aid of a huge concrete banana right on the Pacific Highway, boasts several fun fairs and is especially popular with children. ★ *Byron Bay* **(167/F 2)** is a relaxed small town (pop. 5,000) which attracts mostly young people, particular surfers who come here to enjoy the fabulous surf as well as the local club scene. The town has no less than five hotels for back-packers and is also a popular destination for New Age fans.

Byron Shire Centre
69 Johnston St., Byron Bay, NSW 2481, Tel: 02/66 85 80 50, Fax: 66 85 85 33

Coffs Harbour
Tourist Information Centre
Elizabeth St., Coffs Harbour, NSW 2450, Tel: 02/66 52 15 22, Fax: 66 52 56 74, e-mail: coffsfuture@ coffs.net.au

Port Macquarie
Visitors Information Centre
Clarence/Hay St., Port Macquarie, NSW 2444, Tel: 02/65 83 12 93, Fax: 65 84 15 86, e-mail: vic@ hastings.nsw.gov.au

Port Stephens
Tourist Information Centre
Victoria Parade, Nelson Bay, NSW 2315, Tel: 02/49 81 15 79, Fax:

49 84 18 55, e-mail: tops@hunter link.com.au

LORD HOWE ISLAND / NORFOLK ISLAND

Some 800 km to the northeast of Sydney and approximately in the same latitude as Port Macquarie lies a tiny South Sea island which is part of New South Wales. This crescent-shaped, densely-wooded island is called Lord Howe (**O**) and was created by volcanoes. It is still dominated by two mountains, 875 and 777 m high. Measuring about 12 km in length, it is only a few hundred metres wide in most places – barely enough for a small runway on which light aircraft can land. Once the airport was completed, tourism on this "world heritage" island developed rapidly. As flights are still rather expensive and accommodation is also anything but cheap, Lord Howe Island has remained relatively un-

---

Danger from the Deep

Australia's coastline has a length of 36,735 km, with beaches of beautiful white sand extending for thousands of kilometres. But these beaches also have their perils, so do not jump into the gentle waves when you see fine sand and turquoise water: you might encounter poisonous sea snakes and equally lethal jelly-fish, and huge crocodiles as well as hungry sharks could be lurking for prey off shore. Every year you hear about swimmers being attacked and killed by sharks. In fact, even Australian prime minister Harold Edward Holt is thought to have become the victim of such an attack when he disappeared without a trace in 1967 while swimming in the ocean off Portsea. On the other hand, it is still true that in Australia, as elsewhere, more sharks are eaten by people than the other way round. Whenever you see *'flake'* on the menu of a seafood restaurant, there is one less shark to worry about – in most cases, however, it is either a *gummy* or a snapper shark, neither of which is dangerous to man.

known, retaining its exclusive status. The beaches are narrow with very fine sand. The lagoon, protected by coral reefs, is full of tropical fish, and the subtropical vegetation features plants found only on this island. There are no more than 200 people living here, but their number almost doubles during the peak holiday season around Christmas, when even a policeman is stationed here for a few weeks.

Norfolk Island (**O**), about 8 km long and 5 km wide, is in an even more isolated location way out in the Pacific, some 1500 km away from the mainland. In spite of the great distance, tourism on the island is flourishing. There is a modern airport which can accommodate mid-size jetliners. A particular attraction of the island is the opportunity for duty-free shopping at significantly lower prices than on the mainland. There are no duties on goods, as the island is considered a "territory" and does not belong to any Australian state. The inhabitants also do not pay income tax and have their own postage stamps. The uninhabited island was discovered by James Cook in 1774 and later served as a penal colony for particularly dangerous criminals. In 1856 the descendants of the "Bounty" mutineers were moved from Pitcairn to Norfolk when their crops failed. Some of them later returned to Pitcairn, while others remained on Norfolk Island.

INFORMATION

For Lord Howe Island
Lord Howe Island Tourist Centre, 91 York Street, Sydney, NSW 2000, Tel: 02/92 44 17 77, Fax: 92 62 63 18

For Norfolk Island
Norfolk Island Government Tourist Bureau, P.O. Box 211, Norfolk Island 2899, Tel: 0 67 23/2 21 47, Fax: 2 31 09

GOLD COAST / SURFERS PARADISE

(**167/F 1–2**) Australia's most popular holiday region extends from the northern boundary of New South Wales all the way to Southport, some 65 km from Brisbane, the capital of Queensland. This stretch of the coastline covers almost 32 km of fine sandy beaches. Some of these beaches are shallow and perfectly suited for children, others are pounded by powerful waves ideal for surfers. Each year, more than two million Australians spend their holidays on the Gold Coast, and the area has rapidly developed from fairly modest beginnings to one of the most densely populated regions of Queensland in just a few years. In addition to the many new hotels and apartment buildings now under construction, funfairs and theme parks of all kinds are also springing up everywhere.

The main resort in this holiday region is *Surfers Paradise* (**167/F 2**). The town bears some similarity to the concrete structures which have come to dominate much of Spanish coast. Foreign tourists are relatively rare on the Gold Coast. After all, travellers from Europe or North America are looking for something different when they come to Australia. The only exception are Japanese tour-

ists arriving in jumbo jets. Correspondingly, Japanese companies
are now investing heavily in the
Gold Coast holiday region.

Charlie's
The holiday region is full of
restaurants of all kinds and categories, many of them lining the
Cavill Avenue Mall, a 300 m long
pedestrian zone in the heart of
Surfers Paradise. Where this
walkway meets the beach you'll
find *Charlie's* with tables set out
under colourful umbrellas, serving meals around the clock. *Cavill
Ave Mall, Category 3*

The selection ranges from luxury
accommodation to family apartments with cooking facilities
and even affordable backpacker
hotels.

Bahia Beachfront Apartments
⬧⬧ All rooms with ocean view
and balcony. Well furnished
apartments. *29 rooms, 154 Esplanade, Surfers Paradise, Qld 4217, Tel:
07/55 38 33 22, Fax: 55 92 03 18*

The Sands Apartments
10-storey complex on the beach.
BYO restaurant. *99 Apartments,
40 The Esplanade, Surfers Paradise,
Qld. 4217, Tel: 07/55 39 84 33,
Fax: 55 31 64 90, Category 3 (min-
imum stay: 3 nights)*

Sheraton Mirage Gold Coast
Luxury hotel on a peninsula near
Surfers Paradise with fine beach
and pool. *293 rooms, Sea World Dr.,
Main beach Qld 4217, Tel: 07/55 91
22 99, Fax: 55 91 22 91, Category 1*

Gold Coast
Visitors & Convention Bureau
*Cavill Ave Mall, Surfers Paradise
Qld 4217, Tel: 07/55 38 44 19,
Fax: 55 70 31 44*

Currumbin
Bird Sanctuary   (167/F 2)
A good place to escape from the
tourist clamour. This 20 hectare
bird sanctuary features not only
exotic birds but also a number of
koalas, kangaroos and other animals native to the Australian continent. *8 am–5.30 pm daily*

Dreamworld   (167/E 2)
Dreamworld is a huge pleasure
park a good way inland near
Coomera on the Pacific Highway, a
popular destination for families
with children. The main attractions include one of the longest
roller-coaster rides in the world
and a koala show. All special
shows are included in the price of
the entrance ticket. *9 am–5 pm
daily, Tel: 07/55 53 31 13*

Lamington
National Park   (167/F 2)
The vast, densely wood national
park in a mountainous region
further inland is full of wild
animals and popular with bush-
walkers. The same goes for the
trails in the Green Mountains
and Binna Burra regions. Visitors
can spend the night in one of the
two lodges in the park. Campsites
are also available.

Seaworld   (167/F 2)
On a peninsula called The Spit, at
the far end of the Gold Coast

north of Surfers Paradise, lies Seaworld, the largest marine park in Australia. The principal attractions are trained dolphins and killer whales as well as water-skiing demonstrations etc. All the special shows are included in the admission price. *10 am–5 pm daily, Tel: 07/55 32 10 55*

BRISBANE / QUEENSLAND

☛ **City Map inside back cover**

(**167 / E–F 1**) The capital of Queensland (pop. 1.3 million) lies some 800 km north of Sydney in a subtropical region with a pleasant climate and more than seven hours of sunshine per day on the average. In the last decade this city, which used to be mocked as a pensioners' metropolis, has developed into a flourishing commercial centre. First founded in 1824, Brisbane even gained worldwide renown when it hosted the 1988 World Fair. Following the expansion of the international airport, the city quickly became one of the major air traffic hubs on the Australian continent competing with Melbourne, the second-largest Australian airport after Sydney. Brisbane lies some 25 km upstream from the mouth of the Brisbane River. In spite of this proximity to the ocean, the city does not have the appearance of a seaport. Due to its favourable location it is an ideal starting point for day trips to the Gold Coast and the Sunshine Coast or to the national parks up in the mountains. Next to the city centre, the most interesting districts of Brisbane are Fortitude Valley and Paddington where a

lively restaurant and club scene has developed around local artists' colonies. Brisbane has a relatively good public bus system, although most buses operate only to 11 pm at night (and,, indeed, 7 pm in the evening on Sundays). An information centre for bus services is found in the underground bus station underneath the Myer Centre by the Queen Street Mall *(Mon–Fri 8.30 am–5 pm)*. A passenger ferry has been established on the Brisbane River.

VIEWS OF THE CITY

City Hall Tower
〽 There is an elevator leading up to the tower of the old Town Hall which is now surrounded by skyscrapers. The historic building now houses a collection of paintings. *Adelaide St.*

Mount Coot-tha
〽 From the peak of this mountain, some 6 km outside the city, you can enjoy a wonderful view of Brisbane as well as the coastline and the surrounding mountains. Also worth a visit are the botanical garden and the nearby restaurant. *Tel: 07/33 69 99 22*

SIGHTS

Lone Pine Sanctuary
This wildlife park a little way upriver on *Jesmond Rd., Fig Tree Pocket,* features kangaroos and koala bears. A good way to reach it is by boat which leaves across from the Arts Centre. Lone Pine is also accessible by car and by bus. The Lone Pine Sanctuary opens *9 am–5 pm daily* and is equipped with barbecue facilities. *Tel: 07/33 78 13 66*

South Bank

Next to the *Art Gallery* and the *Performing Arts Centre* on the other side of the river, the site of the World Expo 88 has been re-developed with a number of public facilities such as a beach, a rainforest park, a butterfly house and several restaurants. The South Bank is accessible by train or by car across one of the bridges, but the fastest way to get there from the city centre is to take the small ferry (pedestrians only) across the River. The *South Bank is open 10 am–10 pm daily.*

Walking tour of the city

The city centre has a number of historic buildings from the 19th and early 20th century scattered between the high-rise buildings. To explore the city centre on foot, you should start from the pedestrian zone in *Queen Street* and head for nearby *City Hall* (1920–30). This major landmark (and symbol of Brisbane) now houses a museum with art gallery *(Mon–Fri 10 am–5 pm).* Nearby, between city centre and the riverbank, the former *Treasury* has been transformed into a gambling casino. A few blocks to the south, in a bend in the river, are the old *Botanical Garden,* the *Parliament Building* of 1865 and the *Old Government House* (1860). The latter is now the home of the *National Trust of Queensland (Tel:*

Brisbane Mall, a bustling shopping street for pedestrians only

07/32 29 17 88) which publishes a very informative booklet (in English) describing a walking tour through the historic centre of Brisbane.

RESTAURANTS

Breakfast Creek Wharf
★ ❂ Brisbane's most popular seafood restaurant is situated right on Breakfast Creek some 4 km away from the city centre. The speciality of this restaurant are the extremely tasty mud crabs – some Australians travel for miles to enjoy this delicacy. The restaurant itself is rather expensive, but there is also a reasonably-priced take-away section. *192 Breakfast Creek Rd., Tel: 07/33 52 24 51, Category 2*

Port Office Hotel
✗ Popular meeting place for mostly young people. Affordable but not all that ambitious cuisine. Thu-Sun live jazz as well as other music. *38 Edward St., Tel: 07/32 21 00 72, Category 3*

HOTELS

Bellevue Hotel
Middle-category hotel in a central location with very good furnishings and service. *104 rooms, 103 George St., Brisbane, Qld 4000, Tel: 07/32 21 60 44, Fax: 32 21 74 74, Category 2–3*

Sheraton Brisbane
First-class hotel in the heart of the city, catering for both tourists and businessmen. The pricey "Tower" floors offer luxury service. *435 rooms, 249 Turbot St., Brisbane, Qld 4000, Tel: 07/38 35 35 35, Fax: 38 32 47 41, Category 1*

ENTERTAINMENT

✗ *Tracks Nightspot* at the corner of George and Adelaide Streets is currently the "top" club in the city for young people. Similarly popular is the *Brisbane Underground* at the corner of Hale and Caxton Streets in the Paddington district.

The *Mall* on Queens Street is a busy spot until well into the night – although the culinary offerings are far from exciting. By contrast, many good restaurants are found in *Brunswick Street* in the district of Fortitude Valley. Also recommended are the *Given* and the *Latrobe Terrace in Paddington* – one of the liveliest parts of the city at night.

INFORMATION

Brisbane
Visitors and Convention Bureau
City Hall, King George Sq., Brisbane, Qld 4001, Tel: 07/32 21 84 11, Fax: 32 29 51 26

Queensland
Government Travel Centre
This office provides not only information about all the tourist regions in the state of Queensland but also about special excursion flights out to the Great Barrier Reef. *196 Adelaide St., Brisbane, Qld 4000, Tel: 07/38 33 52 55, Fax: 32 21 53 20*

SURROUNDING AREA

Glasshouse Mountains   (167/E 1)
These volcanic mountains, now turned into protected reserves, were named by James Cook for their unusual shape. To the Aborigines they have become the subject of many legends.

One of Queensland's picturesque beaches

Moreton National Park   (167/F 1)
This national park on Moreton Island, a vast wilderness reserve, is dominated by Mount Tempest, at 280 m one of the highest sand-dunes in the world. The island is part of Moreton Bay some 50 km off the coast at Brisbane. There is a daily boat service from Brisbane as well as ferry service from several coastal towns in the area.

North Stradbroke Island   (167/F 1)
This island in Moreton Bay has a population of about 2,300. Only the northern part of the sand island is accessible as the southern part is commercially exploited by the construction industry as a source of building sand. But "Straddie" as the densely wooded island is fondly called, does have some splendid isolated beaches and hiking trails. *Dunwich,* the largest settlement on the island, was established in 1828 as a quarantine station. The cemetery bears witness to the fact that a cholera epidemic once claimed a total of 28 victims on the island.

Sunshine Coast (**167/F 1**)

This stretch of the coastline north of Brisbane has not yet been as fully developed for tourism as the Gold Coast. The main towns in this region are *Maroochydore (Tourist Information Centre Tel: 07/54 79 15 66)* and the somewhat more elegant *Noosa Heads (Tel: 07/54 47 98 88)* which is situated near the cliffs of Noosa National Park. If you go to *Caloundra,* 70 km north of Brisbane, you can see a replica of Captain Cook's ship "Endeavour" open for visitors *9 am–4.45 pm daily, Tel: 07/41 92 12 78.* In addition, the Sunshine Coast is a good point of departure for trips to *Fraser Island,* the largest sand island in the world. The island is 120 km long and has more than 100 lakes; it was recently declared a Unesco World Heritage Site. As there are no paved roads, you can only explore the countryside in a vehicle with four-wheel drive. Before you take your vehicle onto the ferry, however, a special permit is required which can be obtained from the municipal authorities at *Hervey Bay* and in the *River Heads* trading post. There are several places on the mainland where you can rent a four-wheel drive vehicle. At the *Visitors Centre in Eurong (Tel: 07/41 27 91 28)* you can get maps showing the extensive network of nature trails on the island. There are several hotels of different categories and many campsites. On the island you can see numerous free-roaming dingoes, a kind of wild dog indigenous to Australia.

Whitsunday Islands (158/B–C 1–2)

〰 These 70 or so islands – often erroneously regarded as being part of the Great Barrier Reef – include some of the most popular holiday destinations for Australians. Thanks to the modern airport on Hamilton Island which can accommodate mid-size jetliners, holidaymakers can book direct flights from the major cities in southern Australia. In addition, the islands are accessible from many places on the continent by ferries, speedboats, small planes as well as helicopters. Many of the islands have been turned into nature reserves, but camping is permitted on most of them.

The biggest tourist centre is on *Hamilton Island* (**158/B 2**). This island can accommodate more than 1000 holiday makers and offers a wide variety of activities and a fun-oriented atmosphere. *Package tours offer the best deal. Tel: 07/49 46 91 44, Category 1–2.*

Hayman Island (**158/B 1**) is owned by a large airline company. There is only one – rather expensive – holiday complex on the island. Guests are picked up on Hamilton Island by a luxury yacht. *Tel: 07/49 46 93 33, Category 1*

Lindeman Island (**158/B 2**) is a quiet, not much frequented resort island with airstrip. *Tel: 07/49 46 91 00, Category 2*

NORTH QUEENSLAND/ CAIRNS

(**151/E–F 2–6**) The tropical section of the coastline roughly extends from Townsville (pop. 100,000) via Cairns (pop. 70,000) and the small, historic settlement of Cooktown to the tip of the largely uninhabited Cape York peninsula, where an isolated lodge in the wilderness welcomes visitors.

This more than 1,200 km long stretch of the coast is famous for its beaches, for the deep-sea fishing (especially for the blue marlin), and most of all, for the Great Barrier Reef.

In the competition for the tourist trade in North Queensland, *Cairns* is increasingly becoming more attractive than Townsville although the latter is much larger. In the last few years, however, *Townsville* (**158/A 1**) is making new efforts to win a larger share of the profitable tourist business. The biggest attraction the city has to offer is without a doubt the *Great Barrier Reef Wonderland,* a huge aquarium complex built in 1988 for some 20 million Australian dollars to celebrate the country's bicentennial *(Flinders St., 9 am– 5 pm daily, Tel: 07/47 72 71 22).* The complex also includes an omnimax cinema with a gigantic screen. Directly in front of the aquarium is a pier from which the boats depart for *Magnetic Island* (**158/A 1**); this island on the Reef is partly protected as a nature reserve. Other attractions in Townsville include a number of museums on the maritime history of the region as well as on the Australian army and air force *(info: Townsville Enterprise, 3 The Strand, Townsville, Qld 4810, Tel: 07/47 71 30 61, Fax: 47 71 43 61).*

Like Cairns (**151/F 5**), Townsville also has an international airport, but Cairns has the advantage of much better access to the Great Barrier Reef. As a result, deep-sea fishermen from all over the world descend on Cairns every year at the start of the ★ marlin season. The otherwise rather sleepy community has recently begun to accommodate this flood of visitors by building new hotels and entertainment facilities. The *Museum* at the *Art School* (1907) and *Rusty's Bazar* with its Saturday morning market have become tourist attractions. The backpackers who flock to Cairns by the thousands each year come mainly to take a trip out to the Reef. Other popular destinations for young visitors are the nearby rain forests and the almost uninhabited *Cape York* (**151/E 2**), the northernmost point on the Australian continent.

RESTAURANTS

Backpackers Restaurant

★ As Cairns has become a meeting place for young travellers from all over the world, "Backpackers" is always crowded although the quality of the food leaves something to be desired. *24 Shield St., Cairns, Qld 4870, Tel: 07/40 51 93 23, Category 3*

Somewhere Nice

This restaurant, once awarded the distinction of being the best BYO in North Queensland, offers light Australian cuisine and seating on the balcony and in the garden. *81 Bundock St., Townsville, Qld 4810, Tel: 07/47 72 47 65, Category 2–3*

HOTELS

Beach House Motel

Close to the city centre and right on the beachfront road. *26 rooms, 66 The Strand, Townsville, Qld 4810, Tel: 07/47 21 13 33, Fax: 47 71 68 93, Category 2*

Radisson Plaza

This luxury hotel is not far from the Esplanade, the main boule-

A continent of extremes

Australia is truly a hot continent. In five of its seven states, temperatures of more than 50 degrees Celsius have been recorded. At the other end of the scale, the Snowy Mountains once had a low of – 22 degrees Celsius. And although Australia is the second driest continent after Antarctica, rainfall of up to 96 centimetres within a single day has been reported in Queensland.

vard of Cairns, and directly on the marina which becomes the centre of town during the deep sea fishing season in autumn. *217 rooms, Warf St., Cairns, Qld 4870, Tel: 07/40 31 14 11, Fax: 40 31 32 26, Category 1*

Silver Palm

Simple, affordable guest house in the best location. *153 Esplanade, Cairns, Qld 4870, Tel: 07/40 31 60 99, Fax: 40 31 60 94, Category 3*

ENTERTAINMENT

♁ In the evening, the Esplanade is usually quite crowded, mostly with young travellers and backpackers. Accordingly, the waterfront promenade is lined with countless inexpensive restaurants, fast-food places and kiosks offering tickets for tours out to the Reef or into the mountains. In addition, you can also book various sports activities including parachuting, bush-walking and white-water rafting. Thanks to the large number of young holidaymakers, Cairns can also boast an unusually busy nightlife and a lively club scene, considering the small size of the city. Some of the more popular clubs are the *End of the World* and *Troppo's Nonstop Rock*, the latter being open all through the night.

INFORMATION

**Tourism Tropical
North Queensland**
51 The Esplanade, Carins, Qld 4870, Tel: 07/40 51 35 88, Fax: 40 51 01 27

SURROUNDING AREA

Atherton Tableland   (151 / E–F 5)
There is a railway line, now used primarily by tourists, which runs through the lush rain forest to take visitors from Cairns up to the highlands, ending in *Kuranda* some 30 km away. The rocky landscape makes for a fascinating journey, and the station at the end of the line looks rather like a greenhouse with sidings. The small town of Kuranda is gradually developing into a veritable tourist centre with lots of new buildings, but the local *Tjapukai Dance Theatre (Tel: 07/40 42 99 99)* is still one of the best Aboriginal companies in Australia.

Great Barrier Reef   (151 / E–F 2–6)
The largest coral reef in the world lies off the north coast of Australia and is roughly 2,000 km long. Near Cairns and further north, this coral reef runs relatively close to the coast, elsewhere the distance may be up to 60 km. Only very few holiday islands are actually part of the Reef. Most of

A fascinating bird's-eye view of the Great Barrier Reef

them, like the Whitsunday Islands, are situated between the coral banks and the mainland. The best way to explore the wonderful world of the corals is of course by boat. ★ Panorama flights are also available and offer a fascinating bird's-eye view of this huge natural paradise. The Great Barrier Reef is considered to be one of the most beautiful diving and snorkeling areas in the world. Ecologists are worried about the future of the reef, however, which is threatened not only by the ever increasing tourism but also by the crown-of-thorns, a species of starfish which feeds on the corals and thus gradually destroys the reef. An additional concern is the proposed offshore exploration for oil near the Reef which might lead to poisoning of the coral by oil residues.

Some of the Reef islands – especially those further south which are more easily accessible from the mainland harbours – have been developed for tourism, and almost all of them now have runways for light aircraft:

Bedarra Island (**151/F 6**), one of the lesser known and rather exclusive islands, has two small hotel complexes which are accessible from neighbouring Dunk Island. The first is called *Bay Resort, Tel: 07/40 68 82 33,* the second is the *Hideaway Resort, Tel: 07/40 68 81 68. Both are Category 1*

★ *Dunk Island* (**151/F 6**) is a wooded tropical island with an expensive holiday complex *(Tel: 07/40 68 81 99, Category 1).* Most of the island is a nature reserve. Boats leave for Dunk Island from Wongaling Beach and Mission Beach, flights are available from Cairns and Townsville.

Fitzroy Island (**151/F 5**) is not far from Cairns. Popular with divers, most of the island has been turned into a national park. The

Fitzroy Resort (Tel: 07/40 51 95 88) offers basic hotel accommodation as well as rather expensive villas *(Category 1–3).*

Great Keppel Island (**158/C4**) is one of the best known holiday islands in Queensland and offers not just hotels but also a youth hostel *(Tel: 07/49 39 43 41).* Boats to the island depart from *Rosslyn Bay,* but many visitors prefer to fly to Great Keppel from the Rockhampton airport.

Green Island (**151/F5**) is one of the few genuine coral islands. It is not far from Cairns and therefore attracts a lot of day trippers. *Green Island Reef Resort, Tel: 07/ 40 51 46 44, Category 1–2*

Heron Island (**159/D4**) is especially popular with divers and has a relatively large holiday hotel *(Tel: 07/49 78 14 88, Category 1).* Most of the island has been turned into a national park. It is easily reached by boat from Gladstone.

Hinchinbrook Island (**151/F6**), a mountainous island of 635 sq km, has been declared a national park. Aside from a simple but rather expensive hotel *(Tel: 07/40 66 85 85)* there are only campsites for visitors. Boats to the island depart from Cardwell and Lucinda.

Lizard Island (**151/F4**), surrounded by coral gardens, is the northernmost island. The comfortable lodge *(Tel: 07/40 60 39 99, Category 1)* is popular with many celebrities. Most visitors come to the island by light aircraft from Cairns or Port Douglas.

Port Douglas (151/F5)

This small harbour (pop. 3,700) suddenly became a popular holiday destination for the high society in the mid-1980s, when two luxury hotels were constructed here. But the relaxed, easy-going atmosphere of "Port," as the town is usually called for short, also continues to attract young travellers with less padded wallets. Port Douglas is an ideal point of departure for tours of the nature reserves and national parks of the *Mossman Gorge,* on Daintree River and on *Cape Tribulation* further to the north. If you have less time available, you should at least explore the *Rainforest Habitat* in Port Douglas, a specially planted rainforest with raised wooden walkways. In the harbour you will find boats offering tours out to the Great Barrier Reef.

Extensive tours with four-wheel drive vehicles take you out to the sparsely populated *Cape York peninsula.* The main destination is usually *Cooktown* (**151/F4**), founded at the spot where James Cook once landed to repair his damaged ship. The small town on the Endeavour River experienced a gold rush in the years 1873 to 1883. Some memorable buildings from that time still survive. Cooktown is hard enough to get to on the largely unpaved roads, but things get really tough on the way to the northern tip of the peninsula where a number of sizable rivers need to be crossed. Even with powerful four-wheel drive vehicles this is often possible only in the early morning hours when the riverbed has not yet been churned up too badly. From the tip of the peninsula you can see the *Torres Strait Islands* (**151/D–F1**) which are part of Australia. Their inhabitants are closely related to the Aborigines. Many Torres Strait Islanders are presently calling for complete independence from Australia.

The homeland of Crocodile Dundee

The wilderness of northern Australia is still largely undeveloped and sparsely populated

The coastline of northern Australia, thousands of kilometres long, is hot and humid and for the most part uninhabited and wild. Wide beaches with fine white sand seem to be perfect for swimming, but the waters are full of crocodiles, sharks, sea snakes and highly poisonous jellyfish. Large sections of the coast consist of impenetrable mangrove swamps – the perfect habitat for salt-water crocodiles. Contrary to their name, however, these "salties" – which can grow to a length of more than six metres – are not limited to the ocean and the brackish waters of the swamps. They are also found in many of the freshwater lakes further inland, along with the Johnston crocodile which pose no threat to man. Following the worldwide success of the film "Crocodile Dundee" shot on the north coast of Australia, the crocs have become the main tourist attraction of the North. There are only three regions here which are competing for the tourist business. Aside from Darwin, the

Made famous by "Crocodile Dundee", these dangerous reptiles can grow up to 6 metres long

capital of the Northern Territory, these are the regions of Kununurra and Broome which are already part of Western Australia.

DARWIN

(149/D2) This city of approximately 90,000 inhabitants has suffered more tragedies than any other city in Australia. In 1942, it was repetedly attacked from the air by Japanese bombers, claiming 243 lives. In 1974, disaster struck again when one of the many hurricanes occuring in the region hit Darwin, causing far more damage than ever before. Cyclone "Tracy" practically devastated the entire area. At the time, the authorities were seriously considering whether to rebuild the city at all or whether to leave it to be reclaimed by the jungle. In the end, Darwin was given a second chance, and a new city was built in modern style, first with massive concrete structures and later, beginning in the 1980s, with more innovative architecture, as seen for example in the casino at Diamond Beach. In the mid-1990s Darwin was the fastest growing city in Australia.

SIGHTS

Aquascene

Each day at high tide, the water brings thousands of fish to Doctor's Gully, a bay at the edge of the city centre. They come here to be fed: visitors can walk out into the water and feed them by hand. For information and a table of the tides you should contact either the *Tourist Office* or *Aquascene (Tel: 08/89 81 78 37).*

Botanic Gardens

In the heart of the largest plantation of tropical palm trees in the southern hemisphere visitors will find, among other attractions, an orchid farm, a small rainforest and wetlands like those found in Kakadu National Park. *The gardens are open 7 am–7 pm daily, the greenhouses 7.30 am–3.45 pm only, Gardens Rd, Tel: 08/89 82 25 11*

Indo-Pacific Marine

An aquarium with living coral reefs but relatively few fish. Very informative, but still somewhat disorganized after moving to the new premises. In the neighbouring new building which houses the *Australian Pearling Exhibition* you can learn all about pearl fishing. *9 am–5 pm daily, in the Wharf Precinct, Tel: 08/89 81 12 94; Pearling Exhibition 10 am–6 pm daily, Tel: 08/89 41 21 77*

A city stroll

A few of the elegant buildings from the past have survived the devastating air raids and cyclones, including the former *Admirality House*, the *Government House*, the *Old Post Office* and the *Old Court House*. One of the new structures is the NT Parliament House. A plan of the city's historical buildings with suggestions for a walking tour is available from the *Tourist information* and the *National Trust of the Northern Territory (Burnett House, Myilly Point, Darwin, NT 0801, Tel: 08/89 12 84 89).*

Victoria Hotel

★ The "Vic," as it is called for short, has been heavily damaged by cyclones three times. It was built in 1894 in the heart of the city near the pedestrian zone. These days you will often hear loud rock music blaring from the balcony on *Smith Street Mall.*

MUSEUMS

Aviation Museum

The huge American B52 bomber was specially restored on Guam for this museum, the youngest in the city, and flown to Darwin in 1990. Next to this giant the other aircraft, including a Mirage jet fighter, appear like toys. The museum shows videos documenting the air battle of Darwin during World War II (in the years 1942/43). *Open 8.30 am–5 pm daily, Stuart Highway, Darwin, Tel: 08/89 47 21 45*

Fannie Bay Gaol Museum

The museum in this former prison, in which two convicts were executed as late as 1952, shows the history, and criminal history, of the city. *10 am–5 pm daily, East Point Rd., Fannie Bay, Tel: 08/89 89 82 11*

Museum & Art Gallery of the NT

The gallery focuses on the art of the Aborigines and their neighbours in Southeast Asia. Biggest attraction of the museum is

"Sweetheart" a stuffed crocodile, the largest ever caught. *Mon–Fri 9 am–5 pm, Sat, Sun 10 am–5 pm, Conacher St., Fannie Bay, Tel: 08/899982 01*

Royal Australian Artillery Museum (War Museum)

Surrounded by a small nature reserve, this museum has been given a fitting place next to a huge old artillery emplacement which is occasionally used today to stage rock concerts. *9.30 am– 4.30 pm daily, East Point, Tel: 08/ 89819702*

RESTAURANTS

Christo's on the Wharf

Christo has moved from the city into a shed at the end of an old commericial wharf. Christo serves wonderful seafood in this relaxed atmosphere, with customers sitting all around an Indonesian boat. Fish'n chips are sold next door to this restaurant. *Tel: 08/ 89818658, Category 2*

Colonial Steakhouse

One of the restaurants serving a speciality of the Northern Territory: buffalo steak. The wild water buffalo, a descendant of imported work animals, used to adorn the country's coat of arms until some years ago. *Smith St. Mall, Tel: 08/89814011, Category 2–3*

Lindsay Street Café

This café has repeatedly won awards for its cuisine. Customers can sit in a tropical garden. *Lunch*

MARCO POLO SELECTION: NORTH COAST

1 Tours to the Tiwis
It is a short flight from Darwin to Bathurst or Melville Island, home of the Tiwi Aborigines who are happy to introduce you to their way of life. You can choose between day trips and longer tours (page 66)

2 Kakadu National Park
Numerous companies in Darwin offer tours to this wonderful national park, including safaris with all-terrain vehicles to observe crocodiles. If you have the time, we recommend taking an extended tour of several days (page 67)

3 Bungle Bungle
The characteristic scenery of this new national park is best seen from the air. Flights in light aircraft can be booked in Kununurra and Halls Creek (page 69)

4 Stars on the silver screen and stars in the sky
Most of the films are re-cent productions, but the cinema is over ninety years old. "Sun Pictures" in Broome is one of the few open-air cinemas which have survived in the Australian tropics and show "flics" (the Australian expression for movies) almost every night (page 71)

Tue–Fri, dinner Tue–Sat, brunch on Sun, BYO, 2 Lindsay St., Tel: 08/ 89 81 86 31, Category 1–2

HOTELS

All Seasons Frontier
A quiet, modern hotel with pool and rooftop restaurant, away from the city centre. The rooms are spacious, the service is friendly. As a special attraction, the hotel frequently organizes traditional *corroborees* (dance festivals) with Aborigines. *84 rooms, 3 Buffalo Court, Tel: 08/89 81 53 33, Fax: 89 41 09 09, Category 2*

Hotel Darwin
Traditional lodging in a tropical-style building. Although the hotel may be in need of renovation in places, it still has a lot of charm. *66 rooms, Herbert St./Esplanade, Tel: 08/89 81 92 11, Fax: 89 81 95 75, Category 2–3*

YMCA Banyan View Lodge
One of twelve backpacker hostels in the city. Clean and safe lodging for young people, offering dormitories as well as a number of single and double rooms. Shared kitchen and barbecue facilities. *40 rooms, 119 Mitchell St., Tel: 08/89 81 86 44, Fax: 89 81 61 04, Category 3*

ENTERTAINMENT

Open-Air Theatre
❖ Looking at the ruins of the massive Town Hall of 1883, you get an idea of the devastation which cyclone "Tracy" wrought in Darwin. The remnants of the Old town Hall in Smith Street now serve as backdrop for an open-air theatre.

Markets
Darwin has two night markets: *Palmerston, Apr–Oct, Fri 5.30–9.30 pm; Mindil Beach, Apr–Oct, Thu 5–10 pm, May–Aug 4–9 pm.* Daytime markets: *Flea Market Rapid Creek, Sun 8 am–2 pm,* and *Patrap Markets, Sat 8 am–2 pm.*

INFORMATION

Darwin Region Tourism Association
38 Mitchell St., Darwin NT 0800, Tel: 08/89 81 43 00, Fax: 89 81 06 53, e-mail: drtainfo@ozemail.com.au

SURROUNDING AREA

Adelaide River (149/D 2)
On the river, which crosses the road shortly before the entrance to Kakadu National Park, there are several boats on an unusual, adventurous course. The crews bait the crocodiles by offering them lumps of meat attached to long fishing rods, and the giant reptiles jump up out of the water to snap greedily at the tasty bait. *65 km southeast of Darwin, Tel: 08/89 88 81 44*

Bathurst and Melville Island (149/D 1–2)
★ These islands off Darwin are inhabited by the Tiwi Aborigines. They offer tours of the island (day trips or extended stays) and introduce visitors to the culture of their tribe.

Crocodile Farm (149/D 2)
On this farm, situated roughly 40 km south of Darwin, approximately 7,000 crocodiles are bred for their skin and meat. *Feeding time is at 2 pm daily, Tel: 08/ 89 88 14 50*

Earth colours dominate the paintings of the Tiwi Aborigines

Kakadu National Park (149/E 2–3)

★ The 20,000 sq km national park is one of the biggest attractions of the "top end" as the region around Darwin is called. The park lies 250 km southeast of Darwin and offers accommodation in hotels and on campsites. The name of the park is derived from the Gagadju tribe of Aborigines. *Bowali Visitor Centre, Kakadu Hwy., Jabiru, NT 0886, Tel. 08/89 38 11 00*

Litchfield National Park (149/D 2–3)

This 146,000-hectare national park some 115 km south of Darwin is famous for its waterfalls and lakes. The bizarre sandstone formations of the *Lost City* in the heart of the park are only reached with rough-terrain vehicles. *Accommodation on campsites only. For information contact the Conservation Commission, Tel: 08/89 89 44 11*

Territory Wildlife Park (149/D 2)

This park was created by the authorities of the Northern Territory in a bushland area about an hour's drive from Darwin. Here you can observe the animals indigenous to the territory from a glazed viewing tunnel and in the barramundi aquarium. There are interesting demonstrations with large birds of prey. *8.30 am–6 pm daily, admission until 4 pm, Cox Peninsula Rd., Berry Springs, Tel: 08/89 88 60 00*

Windows of the Wetland (149/D 2)

〰 Located on a hill in the midst of a tropical landscape, which is flooded by the Adelaide River half the year, a visitors centre illustrates the life cycles in these wetlands. From the upper floor you have a great view across the plain. A visit to the centre is best combined with excursion to the Adelaide River with its jumping crocodiles and to Kakadu National Park. *9 am–5 pm daily, Arnhem Hwy., Beatrice Hill, Tel: 08/89 78 89 04*

KUNUNURRA

(148/C4) This small town (pop. 4,200) was founded in the 1960s and has developed into a kind of tourist centre of the Kimberley region. The main attractions are a nearby lake with a rich birdlife and the huge Argyle reservoir in the hinterland. Kununurra was originally founded in conjunction with an extensive agricultural irrigation project. The project area is easily surveyed from the top of *Kelly's Knob Lookout* not far from the town.

ACCOMMODATION

Desert Inn Backpackers
Well-equipped hostel-type accommodation in the centre of town, ideal for backpackers. The best of the three local hostels. *Tristania St., Tel: 08/91 68 27 02, Fax: 91 68 22 71, Category 3*

Mercure Kununurra
Modern, well-equipped lodging with spacious rooms, laid out like a motel. With a large swimming pool. *60 rooms, Duncan Hwy./ Mesmate Way Kununurra, WA 6743, Tel: 08/91 68 14 55, Fax: 91 68 26 22, Category 2*

INFORMATION

Kununurra Tourist Bureau
Coolibah Dr., Kununurra, WA 6743, Tel: 08/91 68 11 77, Fax: 91 68 25 98

SURROUNDING AREA

Argyle Diamond Mine   **(148/C5)**
This mine, in which the rare pink diamonds and other gems are found, produces one third of all diamonds mined in the world. Organized tours are available for visitors. Since the mine lies more than 200 km south of Kununurra, it is convenient to opt for

The multi-layered rocks in Bungle Bungle National Park are best seen from the air

a tour by light aircraft and to combine it with a visit to Bungle Bungle.

Bungle Bungle   (148/C 5–6)

★ In order to see the strange, banded formations of dark and orange-coloured rock, this national park is best explored from the air. Excursion flights are available from Kununurra and from Halls Creek.

El Questro Station   (148/C 4)

This working ranch in the heart of the mountain region east of Kimberley lies some 100 km west of Kununurra on a side road of the Gibb River Road. The landscape is famous for its many canyons, waterfalls and hot springs. The ranch offers various types of accommodation, from luxury homes to campsites. *Bookings: P.O. Box 909, Banksia St., Kununurra, WA 6743, Tel: 08/ 91 91 17 77*

Halls Creek   (148/B 6)

Halls Creek is a small town on the Great Northern Highway, the road to Broome, and lies some 360 km southwest of Kununurra. The town itself has little to offer, but a few kilometres further on you come to the ruins of a gold-mining town of 1885. And some 150 km south is *Wolf Crater National Park,* accessible by dirt road, where a meteorite once hit the ground, leaving a huge 50 m deep crater which measures no less than 835 m in diameter.

Hidden Valley National Park   (158/C 4)

This small nature reserve lies just outside Kununurra, its main attraction is a spectacular canyon.

There are a number of easy hiking trails through the park.

Lake Argyle   (148/C 4–5)

This man-made reservoir is full of fish which attract lots of anglers, but there are also many crocodiles to watch out for. Boat excursions and a museum devoted to pioneering days. *Accommodation: Lake Argyle Tourist Village, Park Rd., Kununurra, WA 6743, Tel: 08/91 68 73 60, Category 3*

Wyndham   (148/C 4)

This port (pop. 900), situated some 100 km from Kununurra, is one of the oldest towns in the north, being founded more than 100 years ago. Wyndham has recently begun to celebrate its long history by creating a so-called Heritage Trail. Nearby *Three Mile Caravan Park* boasts the biggest boab tree in Australia with a circumference of approximately 25 m. *Wyndham Tourist Association, O'Donnell St., Wyndham Port, WA 6740, Tel: 08/91 61 10 54*

BROOME

(153/E 2) This small, rapidly growing town (pop. 9,000) has won a new lease on life by turning to tourism. Around the turn of the century, Broome ranked as one of the world's leading suppliers of mother-of-pearl. The seashells were harvested from the sea-bed by Asian divers, and many Asian influences are still evident here to this day. Some of the old pearl luggers are still moored at the old jetty, although few of them are still in use. The coast consists of muddy banks, but a new harbour has been built which can accommodate larger sea-going vessels.

Once an important hydroplane base, Broome was attacked by Japanese bombers in 1942. The bombing raids claimed the lives of 70 people. The wrecks of the destroyed hydroplanes can still be seen out in Roebuck Bay at low tide. The tropical town with its relaxed atmosphere has many sites of historic interest which are described in detail in a little booklet published by the town.

SIGHTS

Cable Beach

The finest beach lies about 6 km outside town. If you go out to Gantheaume Point when the tide is extremely low, you may get to see the footprint of a dinosaur. A copy of this footprint has been recreated in concrete on land.

Chinatown

Unfortunately, only a few of the old timber buildings of the Chinese traders have survived in the old town on Carnavon Street and Dampier Terrace. In this neighbourhood you can also find some very good restaurants and pubs.

Cemeteries

A Japanese burial ground and a pioneer cemetery bear witness to the tough times the people had to go through before and during the

Broome: one of the last pearl luggers moored to the pier at low tide

heyday of the pearling industry. The Japanese cemetery has been partially restored.

Broome Historical Society Museum

The museum found a fitting home in the old Customs House on Saville Street. It illustrates both the successes and the difficulties of the pearling industry. *Mon–Fri 10–12 am and 2–4 pm, Sat and Sun 10–12 am only*

RESTAURANT

Roebuck Bay Hotel

This pub is a living reminder of the tough atmosphere which dominated in the pearling days – not for the sensitive visitor, as it is always noisy and sometimes quite rowdy. At the *Pearlers Restaurant* you can dine out in the open. *Carnavon St., Tel: 08/91 92 12 21, Category 2–3*

ACCOMMODATION

Broome's Last Resort

On the edge of town, one of several backpacker lodgings. Dormitories and rooms with two or four beds. *2 Bagot St., Broome, WA 6725, Tel: 08/91 93 50 00, Fax: 91 93 69 33, Category 3*

Intercontinental Cable Beach Club

Luxury resort hotel in a tropical park with two swimming pools, separated from the beach by a relatively quiet road. *84 rooms, Cable Beach Rd., Broome, WA 6725, Tel: 08/91 92 04 00, Fax: 91 92 22 49, Category 1*

Mangrove Motel

Seaside motel with a nice pool. *49 rooms, Dampier Terrace, Broome,* *WA 6725, Tel: 08/91 92 13 03, Fax: 91 93 51 69, Category 2*

ENTERTAINMENT

Sun Pictures

★ In Carnavon Street, in the heart of the Chinatown district, you can't miss the – rather old-fashioned – lights of the *Sun Pictures* cinema which has been in existence since 1916.

It is one of the few surviving open-air cinemas in Australia which are still showing films every day. It is fun to relax in a sunlounger under the stars and watch some of the Hollywood celebrities in action.

INFORMATION

Broome Tourist Office

Great Northern Hwy., Broome, WA 6725, Tel: 08/91 92 22 22, Fax: 91 92 20 63

SURROUNDING AREA

Dampier Peninsula   (153/E 1–2)

A four-wheel drive vehicle is recommended for the road across the peninsula to the Cape Leveque lighthouse some 200 km away. Nearby is *Lombadina*, a settlement of Aborigines which offers its own tourist programme. About halfway there you should stop at *Beagle Bay*, another Aboriginal settlement with a church decorated with mother-of-pearl.

Willie Creek Pearl Farm   (153/E 2)

On this working farm, pearls are cultivated and processed. It is well worth a visit, and tourists are always welcome. The farm is situated less than 40 km from Broome on *Cape Leveque Rd.*

The most isolated metropolis on Earth

The city of Perth is flourishing in the heart of an almost uninhabited wilderness

It is in Perth that almost all tours in Western Australia begin, whether heading north, east or west. The northwest corner of the fifth continent is rich in minerals and has always been mined, and this was the only reason for the development of a few small towns such as Port Hedland and Dampier. Except for that, the northwest would probably have remained as deserted as the major part of the west coast of Australia. It is presumed that this is where the first Europeans landed – Dutchmen who were thoroughly disappointed when they saw the barren land. Further to the south the British later encountered a more agreeable environment. It was here that the most remote metropolis in the world was to be built: Perth, the capital of the huge state of Western Australia, separated from the eastern part of the continent by endless deserts

Victorian architecture in Kalgoorlie, a former gold-mining town

and from Asia by the expanse of the Indian Ocean.

PERTH

☛ City Map inside back cover

(160/C4) Less than 20 km upstream from its mouth, the Swan River widens to form a lake. It was here that the first English settlers landed 1829. Today, the water of this lake reflects the silhouettes of skyscrapers – a towering symbol of the prosperity that Perth enjoys thanks to the mineral riches of Western Australia. The city has a population of about 1.4 million, with another 400,000 living in the huge state of Western Australia, mostly in the cooler southwest. The city of Perth is said to have the best climate in all of Australia. In winter (June–August), the mercury rarely falls below 18°C. In the summer, the temperature frequently reaches 30°C and more, but the afternoons are usually quite pleasant because of the "Fremantle Doctor," a cool wind blowing from the sea. Perth is a metropolis with the relaxed atmosphere of a holiday resort. The beaches on the Indian Ocean are a mere 10 km away – and thus within easy reach after a busy workday in the city. Locals claim that Perth has the finest beaches on the continent, but this claim is of course disputed by all other states in the country.

VIEWS OF THE CITY

Mount Eliza Lookout and Kings Park

★ ☼ Perth may appear like a miniature Manhattan, but is is actually only a few hundred metres from the city to the wilderness: *Kings Park* on a promontory not far from the city centre, and particularly the lookout on Mt. Eliza, afford a panoramic view of the city, the lake, the river and the surrounding countryside. Most of this 404 hectare park is natural bushland and offers a good cross-section of the flora found in the interior. A 17 hectare section of the park has been turned into a botanical garden which is the site of a wild flower show held annually in September, for Western Australia is famous for its spectacular wild flowers. There are numerous trails and bicycle paths in the park which is the home of many rare birds. Next to the car-park, which is not far from the city, is the *Kings Park Information Centre (9.30 am–3.30 pm daily)*. Here you can ask for a schedule of the daily guided tours through this "urban bushland."

SIGHTS

A sense of history

Perth had become rich during the gold rush in Western Australia, and in the 19th century many grand buildings were erected in the city. With the recent discovery of iron ore more money has poured into the city,

MARCO POLO SELECTION: WEST COAST

1 **Rottnest Island**
Swimming, cycling and feeding the quokkas are the main activities on this small island in the Indian Ocean (page 79)

2 **Bushwalking in Kings Park**
If you don't have the time to explore the interior, taking an extended hike through this park outside Perth will give you a good impression of what the Australian wilderness is actually like (page 74)

3 **Dolphins in Monkey Mia**
Wild dolphins will come directly to the tourists, standing in the knee-deep water, to be hand-fed. The feeding sessions are supervised by rangers (page 80)

4 **Prospecting in Kalgoorlie**
A guided tour of the gold mine is already a great experience – but it's more fun to simply rent some equipment and to go out prospecting for yourself (page 83)

The city of Perth has prospered from rich mineral deposits in the area

and again much of it went into the construction of new buildings. In the process, numerous charming old buildings were demolished to make room for huge new office towers. As a result of all this construction, the townscape has become a crazy mix of historic buildings standing right alongside modern high-rise glass structures. The *Old Town Hill* at the corner of Hay Street and Barrack Street is a good example. There is a leaflet available from the *Tourist Information in the Hay Street Mall,* the pedestrian area in the city centre, which tells you in detail how to find some of the historic buildings in the city, such as the *Old Perth Boy's School* (1854), the old *Deanery* (1859), the *Cloisters* (1858), the *Government House* (1859–64), the *Treasury* and the *Old Courthouse.* The majority of these sights are located only a few steps from Hay Street.

Underwater World

This aquarium in the north of the city boasts an impressive collection of more than 200 different species of fish. From the underwater tunnel you can observe sharks and stingrays only an arm's length away. The aquarium also organizes whale-watching excursions to watch the great humpback whales when they pass Fremantle on their way through the Indian Ocean. *9 am–5 pm daily, Hillarys, WA 6025, Boat Harbour, West Coast Dr., Tel: 08/94 47 75 00*

Zoo

The Perth Zoo is situated in a parklike setting on the south side of Swan River Lake. It is easily accessible by car or bus, but on nice days it is more enjoyable to cross the lake by taking the ferry which leaves from Barrack Square in the city centre. In keeping with its environmental concerns the zoo has built a special Conservation

Discovery Centre. There is also a building designed for nocturnal animals where visitors can observe them at their activities during the artificial night. *Opening hours are 10 am–5 pm every day, the nocturnal house is open midday–3 pm daily, South Perth, 20 Labouchere Rd., Tel: 08/93 67 79 88*

MUSEUMS

Perth can boast almost a dozen different museums, *including a Railway Museum (Sun and holidays 1 am–5 pm, Tel: 08/92 79 71 89), a Museum of Childhood with a section on "Victorian Childhood" (Mon–Fri 10 am–3 pm, Sun 2–5 pm, Tel: 08/93 81 11 03), a Telecommuinication Museum (Sat–Sun 2–5 pm, Tel: 08/93 64 70 67) and an Aviation Museum (11 am–4 pm daily, Tel: 08/93 32 44 44).*

Art Gallery of Western Australia
A general collection of art with special emphasis on Australian artists. On weekends there is a regular "Galleria Market" for all sorts of handicrafts, held in front of the museum. *10 am–5 pm daily, James St., Tel: 08/93 28 72 33*

Perth Institute
of Contemporary Art
The Institute has an exhibition hall for modern art and painting. The changing exhibitions are devoted to a wide variety of themes. *10 am–5 pm daily, 51 James St., Tel: 08/92 27 93 39*

Western Australian Museum
This state-run museum features a noteworthy collection of Aboriginal culture, a collection of vintage automobiles and, as a special attraction, a collection of meteorites which have landed on the fifth continent, the heaviest weighing no less than eleven tons. There is also an almost 25 m long skeleton of a whale from the days of commercial whaling. The museum complex also includes the old Perth prison which was in use from 1856 to 1888. *Mon–Fri 10.30 am–5 pm, Sat 1–5 pm, Sun 10.30 am–5 pm, Francis St., Tel: 08/93 28 44 11*

RESTAURANTS

City Center Market
❖ As in other large cities throughout Asia, many of the major cities in Australia have established so-called "food centres" which consist of a number of food stalls offering a variety of different cuisines (Chinese, Mexican, Italian, seafood, vegetarian etc.) grouped around a central area with tables and chairs. One of the best is at Hay Street in the *City Center.* The best days are Thu–Sat, with live music until 9 pm. *Hay St., lower level, Mon–Sat 9 am–9 pm, Category 3*

Fraser's
This popular restaurant in Kings Park offers not just good food but also a fine panoramic view of the city. *Fraser Av., Tue–Sat for lunch and dinner, Sun lunch only, Tel: 08/94 81 71 00, Category 2*

HOTELS

Adelphi Hotel Apartments
Combination hotel (no restaurant) and apartments. No pool. *62 rooms, 130a Mounts Bay Rd., Perth, WA 6000, Tel: 08/93 22 46 66, Fax: 93 22 45 80, Category 3*

Parmelia Hilton
Near the city centre. *327 rooms, Mill St., Perth, WA 6000, Tel: 08/93 22 36 22, Fax: 94 81 08 57, Category 1*

Northbridge YHA Hostel
Hostel with garden in Northbridge, the entertainment district. *42–48 Francis St., Perth, WA 6003, Tel and Fax: 08/93 28 77 94, Category 1*

ENTERTAINMENT

His Majesty's Theatre
This elaborately restored building dates from 1904 and houses the opera and ballet of Western Australia. The Edwardian interior

alone is an attraction well worth visiting. *At the corner of Hay St. and Kings St., Tel: 08/93 22 29 29*

James Street Nightclub
This huge club plays mostly mainstream, rock and sometimes house music. The busiest nights are Fri and Sat. Open from 9 pm until the early morning hours. *139 James St., Northbridge*

INFORMATION

Western Australian Tourist Centre
Corner of Forrest St./Wellington St., Mon–Fri 8.30 am–5.30 pm, Sat 9 am–1 pm, Tel: 08/94 83 11 11, Fax: 94 81 01 90

Wave Rock near Hyden has become a magnet for thousands of tourists

Pinnacles (160/B4)

Namburg National Park is located right on the coast some 260 km north of Perth. Its main attraction are the pinnacles – a field of countless stone pillars and needles up to a height of 5 m rising from a yellow sand desert. Geologists have developed different theories as to how they originated.

Swan River (160/C4)

Several companies are offering boat excursions on Swan River, either down the river to Fremantle or upstream for a visit to the vineyards where you have ample opportunity to taste some of the local wines. In its upper reaches, the Swan River flows through a small national park in a canyon of the Darling Ranges. For details on departure times and ticket prices contact the *Tourist Information in Forrest St.*

Wave Rock (161/D4–5)

One of the best-known natural phenomena in Australia, Wave Rock near Hyden, is reached by bus from Perth (an extended daytour – it's a 700 km round trip). The 15 m high rock with colourful vertical stripes resembles a huge ocean wave which is about to break.

FREMANTLE

(160/C5) Founded in 1829, this old seaport of Perth, some 20 km downriver at the mouth of the Swan River, has managed to preserve its small-town atmosphere in spite of all the shipping activities. There are many charming historic buildings which were carefully restored in 1987 when the city was selected to host the America's Cup yacht race. Fremantle (pop. 24,000) is easily accessible from Perth by railway, bus or excursion boats.

SIGHTS

Walking tour

The small city centre is perfect for a "historic" walking tour. The best place to start is the *Round House* at Arthur Head point, an old stone building of 1831 which is actually not round but has twelve corners. It once served as a prison. There are many noteworthy buildings dating from the turn of the century, the days of the gold rush in Western Australia, such as the church of *St. John's* (1882), the old *Town Hall* (1887) or the old *Railway Station* (1907). *Details are found in the brochure for a historic tour of the city available from the Tourist Information Office.*

MUSEUMS

Fremantle History Museum

This remarkable collection on the whaling industry and on the history of the city and the state is housed in a former asylum which was originally built by British convicts in the mid-19th century. *Mon–Thu 10.30 am–5 pm, Fri–Sun 1–5 pm, Finnerty St., Tel: 08/9430 79 66*

Maritime Museum

The main attraction of this fascinating museum on naval history, housed in a building dating from 1852, is the salvaged wreck of the Dutch vessel "Batavia" which sank off Fremantle in 1629. Restoration is still in progress. *The collec-*

tion is open Mon–Thu 10.30 am–5 pm and Fri–Sun 1–5 pm. At Victoria Quai you can see a collection of historic boats and models commemorating the America's Cup races under the heading of "Sails of the Century" *1–5 pm daily, Cliff St., Tel: 08/93 35 82 11*

RESTAURANT

Ocean Room
Top-rated restaurant in the ocean resort of Scarborough Beach, north of Fremantle. The restaurant is part of the Observation City Resort Hotel (built especially for the America's Cup races). Excellent seafood. *The Esplanade, Scarborough, WA 6019, Tel: 08/92 45 10 00, Category 1*

HOTEL

Fremantle Esplanade Hotel
This comfortable, well-furnished hotel close to the old town centre is popular with conference delegates. *140 rooms, 46 Marine Tce., Fremantle, WA 6160, Tel: 08/94 30 40 00, Fax: 94 30 45 39, Category 2*

INFORMATION

Fremantle Tourist Bureau
William St. at the corner of Adelaide St., Mon–Fri 9 am–5 pm, Sat 9 am–1 pm, Sun 10 am–3 pm, Tel: 08/94 31 78 78, Fax: 94 31 78 20

SURROUNDING AREA

Rottnest Island   (160/C 4–5)
★ ✿ This island is easily reached from Perth by light aircraft or by boat (from the Barrack St. jetty). Less expensive are the island ferries from Fremantle which depart from their moorings near the railway bridge across the harbour. The island acquired its name in 1696 when Dutch explorers, confronted with quokkas – a kind of miniature kangaroo native to the island – mistook them for rats. Affectionately called "Rotto" by local residents, the island, some 19 km off Fremantle, was once used as a prison for Aborigines and is now a popular holiday resort. The best way to explore the island, which is 11 km long and 5 km wide, is by bicycle (rentals available). Glass-Bottom boats and a special vessel with windows below the waterline offer a good way to see the coral reefs and the wrecks of many ships which sank off the island. The small island museum tells their fate in detail. A hotel and a holiday complex are available for longer stays. The Tourist Information Centre is at Thomson Bay pier where the boats from Perth and Fremantle arrive. *Rottnest Island, WA 6161, 9 am–4 pm daily, Tel: 08/94 32 91 11*

EXMOUTH

(152/A 5) If there still are "insider tips" for Australia, one of them would certainly be the small town of Exmouth (pop. 3,200) which was founded as late as 1967 near a U.S. military installation. Exmouth is situated some 1,200 km north of Perth on a peninsula which marks the northwestern tip of Australia. It is dominated by the Cape Range mountains whose spectacular canyons and great beaches have been turned into a national park. At the coast this park borders directly onto Nigaloo Marine Park whose Ningaloo coral reef is "only" 260 km long and hence much smaller than the Great Barrier Reef, but hardly less beautiful. A unique attraction are the whalesharks which gather here in large numbers every March. Marine biologists know of no other place where such a spectacle can be witnessed. This species of fish, the biggest in the world, is quite harmless and very gentle. As they tend to swim close to the surface in the vicinity of the reef, it is possible to approach them at close range and to dive and even swim among them. Several companies offer boat excursions – although not exactly cheap – to watch these fish which can grow to a length of up to 18 m.

SIGHTS

Milyering Visitor Centre
Constructed of compacted clay and powered by solar energy, this Visitor Centre is situated in the heart of the National Park.

As the only access road runs around the cape, it is a 52 km drive from Exmouth to the Centre which has numerous displays dealing with the creation and history of the reef and the mountains as well as the local fauna. *10 am–4 pm daily except Tue and Sat, Tel: 08/99 49 28 08*

Vlaming Lighthouse
↘ This lighthouse, which dates from 1912, is open to visitors from April to October. For details of the opening hours contact the Exmouth Tourist Office. In front of the lighthouse is an abandoned radar installation from World War II. From Vlaming Head you have a good view of the beaches, the reef and the radio antennas of

the naval communications system. The tallest mast is 388 m high. The former U.S. Navy base nearby is now used by the Australian Navy.

RESTAURANT

Whalers Restaurant
Simple but very tasty food and outside seating on a terrace. Open from morning till night. *5 Kennedy St., Tel: 08/99 49 24 16, Category 3*

HOTEL

Potshot Resort Hotel
New building with comfortable rooms. Self-service restaurant with poolside tables. *45 rooms, Murat Rd., Exmouth, WA 6707, Tel: 08/99 49 12 00, Fax: 99 49 14 86, Category 2*

INFORMATION

Exmouth Tourist Bureau
Maidstone Crescent, Exmouth, WA 6707, Tel: 08/99 49 11 76, Fax: 99 49 14 41

MONKEY MIA

(160/A 1) ★ It is a matter of dispute how this bay got its name, as it is famous not for monkeys but for other animals – namely wild dolphins which repeatedly come close to the beach every morning to be fed by hand. This unusual spectacle is closely monitored by wildlife rangers who also run an Information Centre which provides details on the life of the dolphins. The bay is situated on one of the two peninsulas which form Shark Bay, most of which has been declared a Unesco World

Feeding dolphins by hand at Monkey Mia

Heritage Site. A part of the area is known as *François Peron National Park.* The main town in the region is Denham, a sea resort. To get there, turn off the North West Coastal Hwy. at Overlander Roadhouse.

SIGHTS

Hamelin Pool
Some 27 km beyond the Overlander Roadhouse is a turn-off which takes you to the telegraph station at Hamelin Pool. Dating from 1884, the building now houses a small museum which also has a display explaining the stromatolites found in nearby Hamelin Pool: For around 2000 or 3000 million years, microorganisms in the bay have been forming small, mushroom-like rocks. This phenomenon, which is thought to be one of the first forms of life on our planet, can only be witnessed in very few places. The telegraph station also houses a pleasant little café.

INFORMATION

Shark Bay Tourist Centre
83 Knight Tce., Denham, WA 6537, Tel and Fax: 08/99 48 12 53

KALGOORLIE

(**161/E3**) Founded more than 100 years ago at the height of the biggest goldrush in Australia, Kalgoorlie and its twin city of Boulder (total pop. 26,000) are still important mining centres. On Golden Mile, one of the richest veins of gold in the world, the precious metal is still mined. Built in the middle of the desert in Victorian style, Kalgoorlie is also a thriving tourist centre. Day excursions from Perth are only possible by air, as it is 600 km away. But as the famous "Indian-Pacific" also stops in Kalgoorlie on its way across the continent, many rail passengers take the opportunity to stop off. The goldrush began when Paddy Hannan and two fellow Irishmen first discovered gold here in 1893. A statue was erected in his honour on Kalgoorlie's main street. It shows him generously dispensing from his pouch something that was almost as precious as gold in those days – namely water. It was only after a brilliant engineer named C. Y. O'Connor constructed a 563 km pipeline through this arid region in 1903, that Kalgoorlie really started to flourish. Today, O'Connor's water tank on top of Mount Charlotte has become a major tourist attraction, enhanced by the fact that the mountain offers a fabulous view of the city and the gold fields.

SIGHTS

Hannan's North

The goldmine is still in operation today, but only as a tourist attraction. The tours of the mine are mostly conducted by former miners. The museum complex has been built directly above the main vein of Golden Mile, and there is a light railway which takes visitors through the extensive mining area. This interesting tour also includes the casting of an actual gold bar. Guided tours of the museum complex are being offered at least four times a day. *Meekatharra Hwy., Tel: 08/90 91 40 74*

Historic walking tour

Most of the historic buildings from Kalgoorlie's heyday are located on Hannan Street. The street was built unusually wide to allow camel caravans to turn here. The town centre is dominated by the post office, the town hall and several impressive hotels and pubs with nice wrought-iron balconies. The neighbouring town of Boulder also features similar but smaller Victorian buildings such as Boulder Block (there is a public bus service to Boulder). The tourist information office has prepared detailed brochures for two carefully worked-out historic walking tours (4 km in Kalgoorlie, 3 km in Boulder).

Loopline Railway

"Rattler" was the name the miners gave the rattling railway which took them back and forth between the different goldmines. Today this train only carries tourists. The tour with commentary along the "Golden Mile" takes about one hour. Beverages and pastries are served in one of the cars. *Departures from Boulder Station, Burt St., 10 am daily, Sun and holidays also at 11.45 am, Tel: 08/90 93 30 55*

MUSEUMS

Eastern Goldfields Historical Society

Exhibits on the history of gold mining in the region are housed in the former railway station at Boulder, dating from 1897. The museum also has reproductions of vintage photographs for sale. *9–12 am daily, Tel: 08/90 93 11 57*

Museum of the Goldfields

The *British Arms,* arguably the smallest pub in all of Western Australia, is now part of the museum which not only shows an impressive collection of photographs and relics from the gold rush era but also features exhibits on the once profitable search for sandalwood. *10 am–4.30 pm, at the north end of Hannan St., Tel: 08/90 21 19 66*

The Kalgoorlie gold mine is now a major tourist attraction

RESTAURANT

Palace Hotel
Dating from 1897, this hotel used to be the epitome of luxury. Today the rooms provide only basic furnishings, but the pub is still very popular. The hotel restaurant serves not only à-la-carte menus but also a variety of counter meals. *Hannan/Maritana St., Tel: 08/90 21 27 88, Category 3*

HOTEL

Railway Motel
Medium-class establishment. A restored railway hotel of 1897 with new wings, built at the station where the "Indian Pacific" stops. Reopened 1997. *71 rooms, 51 Forrest St., Kalgoorlie, Tel: 08/90 88 00 00, Fax: 90 91 85 86, Category 2*

INFORMATION

Kalgoorlie Tourist Bureau
250 Hannan St., Kalgoorlie, WA 6430, Tel: 08/90 21 19 66, Fax: 90 21 21 80

SURROUNDING AREA

Coolgardie   (161 / E 4)
This town was built in the desert in 1892 following the discovery of gold 40 km west of Kalgoorlie. 15,000 people lived here at one time. Today, there are no more than 700, and Coolgardie has almost become a ghost town, kept alive by tourism only. The railway station (1896), three museums and the old cemetery are the main attractions. *For information call the Tourist Bureau, Bayley St., Tel: 08/90 26 60 90*

Washing gold
★ In Kalgoorlie, you can rent electronic metal detectors as well as old-fashioned hoes and pans if you want to try your luck and look for gold yourself. Local tourist agencies also organize special gold prospecting tours. If you plan to set out on your own you need to get a licence which you can obtain for just a few dollars at the *Mines Department* in Brookham Street.

ALBANY

(**161/D 6**) The huge natural harbour of King George Sound was the reason why Albany, in the southwest corner of the continent, became the first European settlement in western Australia. As early as 1826 the British first established themselves on this bay which served as an important coal station for their steamships before embarking on the long voyage across the Indian Ocean. Before that, the bay had been used mostly by whalers. Today, Albany (pop. 19,000) has become a fairly quiet town which is kept alive by memories of the past – and by the tourists.

VIEW

✤ *Mount Clarence,* easily accessible via Apex Drive, offers a fine panoramic view of the city and King George Sound. On the summit is an impressive monument erected in honour of the Desert Mounted Corps, a cavalry unit of World War II which was transported from Albany to North Africa.

MUSEUMS

Old Goal & Museum
This old prison, built in 1851, has recently been turned into a museum of folklore and local history. *10 am–4.45 pm daily, Stirling Tce., Tel: 08/98 41 14 04*

The Residency Museum
The official residence of the representative of the British Crown was built around 1850. Today it houses a museum on regional history, concentrating on shipping in particular with a replica of the brig "Amity" which originally brought the first settlers to the area. *10 am–5 pm daily, Residency Rd., Tel: 08/98 41 48 44*

Strawberry Hill Farmhouse
Established in 1836, this government farm has been furnished in a variety of historic styles. The willow at the entrance is said to be an offshoot of the tree planted on Napoleon's grave on St. Helena. *10 am–5 pm daily, Middleton Beach Rd., Tel: 08/98 41 37 35*

ACCOMMODATION

Frederickstown Motel
On a slope above the city. *34 rooms, 41 Frederick St., Albany, WA 6330, Tel: 08/98 41 16 00, Fax: 98 41 86 30, Category 2*

INFORMATION

Albany Tourist Bureau
Old Railway Station, Proudlove Parade, Albany, WA 6330, Tel: 08/98 41 10 88, Fax: 98 42 14 90, Mon–Fri 8.30 am–5.30 pm, Sat, Sun 10 am–5 pm

SURROUNDING AREA

Whale World   (161/D 6)
The whaling station lies about 20 km outside the city. When it closed in 1978 it was turned into a whaling museum. Tours with former whalers as guides are offered at irregular times. *9 am–5 pm daily, Frenchman Bay Rd., Tel: 08/98 44 40 21.* Not far away on the coast are some interesting rock formations, including a natural stone bridge and "blowholes" where incoming waves shoot fountains of sea water skyward.

Australia's megastar

When asked about the most famous women in Australia, most people will probably think of opera singer Joan Sutherland or of Collen McCollough, the author of the 'Thornbirds', or even the famous swimmer Dawn Fraser. Asking the same question in Australia, however, you may get a surprising answer: The most popular lady down under is television personality Edna Everage, the star of a satirical comedy show. This self-styled "megastar" is actually a man, by the way: comedian Barry Humphries.

ESPERANCE

(161/F5) This pleasant resort on the south coast with magnificent beaches – even by high Australian standards – is almost unknown abroad. The ocean of the south coast is cooler than elsewhere, however, and only suitable for swimming in summer. During the goldrush in the late 19th century Esperance became a busy port, but today the city (pop. 7,500) relies mainly on agriculture in the surrounding area and on tourism. Just off the coast is the Recherche Archipelago with more than 100 islands.

SIGHTS

Great Ocean Drive

This 36 km circular drive offers many different views of the impressive coastline with its white sand dunes. On the inland side it takes you past Pink Lake which owes its name to a unique species of algae.

Municipal Museum

This colourful museum is chock full of curious items. The showpieces of the collection are the remains of the U.S. space station "Skylab" which crashed in Australia in 1979, six years after its launch, not far from Esperance. *1.30–4.30 pm daily, at the intersection of James St./Dempster St., Tel: 08/90 71 15 79*

RESTAURANT

Gray Starling

This BYO restaurant makes you feel at home, almost like a private house. Outside seating available. Good food and very reasonable prices. *126 Dempster St., Tel: 08/90 71 58 80, Category 2*

HOTEL

Bay of Isles

Comfortable motel on the oceanfront promenade. With spacious rooms, swimming pool and heated whirlpool. *63 rooms, 32 The Esplanade, Esperance, WA 6450, Tel: 08/90 71 39 99, Fax: 90 71 38 00, Category 2*

INFORMATION

Esperance Tourist Bureau

The tourist bureau is located in one of the huts in the historic museums village; the others house arts and crafts workshops and stores as well as a restaurant. *Mon–Fri 8.45 am–5 pm, Sat–Sun 9 am–5 pm, Dempster St., Tel: 08/90 71 23 30, Fax: 90 71 45 43*

From the Nullarbor Plain to Adelaide

Great wine and great art are the major attractions of southern Australia

The south coast of Australia is as impressive as it is deserted. At the *Great Australian Bight,* long stretches of the dry and barren land drop down almost vertically to the sea. This is a rather inhospitable landscape, and there are very few petrol stations and rest stops along this section of Highway 1 which winds its way around the entire continent. Even the railway, running further inland, passes only a few scattered houses, most of them owned by railway employees. But the people in western and southern Australia have high hopes for the development of tourism in this area. The spectacular rugged coast, the whale watching opportunities and the extended network of caverns underneath the seemingly endless limestone plains are to be developed into major tourist at-

A nostalgic sight: one of the last streetcars rattling along on its way to Glenelg, a beach-front suburb of Adelaide

tractions. The only populated areas are at the edges of this barren land: around Albany to the west, on Spencer Gulf to the east, and of course around Adelaide, the capital of South Australia.

ADELAIDE

☛ **City Map inside back cover**

(164/C5) Australia's youngest metropolis (pop. 1,100,000) is best known for its active cultural life, its renowned festival, its parks and its relaxed way of life with great culinary delights. Founded in 1836, the capital of the state of South Australia was laid out in a regular pattern with lavish expanses of green along the Torrens River. It is approximately 10 km from Adelaide to the mouth of the river. Adelaide is also the administrative centre for the industrial districts further north and west on Spencer Gulf. A "high-technology park" known as *Multi-Function-Polis,* supported by federal funding and planned and financed with Japanese aid, will be built on the edge of Adelaide. It will bring together research facilities for telecommunication and information technology, education and environmental management. Construction is estimated to cost around A$ 250 million, but no one knows when the project is actually going to be launched – the beginning of work has been delayed several times already.

VIEW

Light's Vision

↘ This vista point on Montefiore Hill on the north bank of Torrens River offers a great view of the city. It was named after Colonel William Light, the man who planned the city.

SIGHTS

Botanical Gardens

Thanks to the Mediterranean climate, Adelaide is a veritable city of flowers. The vast Botanical Garden (16 hectares) not far from Ayers House boasts a huge variety of native and exotic plants. *Mon–Fri 7 am–7 pm, Sat, Sun 9 am–7 pm, in winter to 5.30 pm, Tel: 08/82 28 23 11*

Festival Centre Complex

The Festival Centre, a white complex designed in modern style, standing in the park on the bank of Torrens River, was built in 1974. Every two years (in even years) it hosts Australia's finest international festival of music, theatre and fine arts. *Mon–Sat*

MARCO POLO SELECTION: SOUTH COAST

1 Telegraph Station
There is not much left of this once busy outpost of communication, but it is interesting to see how the constantly moving sand dunes are gradually reclaiming the deserted terrain (page 94)

2 Wadlata Outback Centre
Sophisticated videos and straightforward displays have been combined in this vivid presentation of the outback – particularly helpful if you plan to explore the interior of the continent by following the asphalt band of the Stuart Hightway (page 95)

3 Rundle Street
This street in Adelaide is lined with restaurants – a wonderful opportunity to sample the excellent wines produced down under by indulging in a "pub crawl" (page 91)

4 Kangaroo Island
The main attraction of this big island south of Adelaide is not so much the kangaroos, as you might think, but the colony of huge sea lions living on the south shore. To avoid being attacked, use caution when you approach them! (page 91)

Busy all year round: the Arts Festival Centre

10 am–4 pm, guided tours almost every hour, King William Rd., Tel: 08/82 16 87 13

Glenelg

The last remaining tram in Adelaide runs from the city centre to the lively sea resort of Glenelg *(departure from Victoria Sq., travel time 25 min.).* It was here that South Australia was founded in 1836, when a proclamation was read aloud under an old eucalyptus tree which still stands today. Brochures for a historic walking tour are available in Bay World opposite the town hall. A replica of the "Buffalo", which brought the first settlers is moored in the harbour (restaurant on board).

North Terrace

Adelaide's stateliest street runs parallel to Torrens River. Most of the city's historic buildings are found on this street: The elegant *railway station* of 1929 now houses a gambling casino, *Government House* is in a park at the corner of King William Street, and at the east end of North Terrace the basalt structure of *Ayers House* (1846) is open to visitors. This former residence of the prime minister, now the headquarters of the *National Trust of South Australia,* is open *Tue–Fri 10 am–4 pm and Sat, Sun 2–4 pm (Tel: 08/82 33 16 55).*

Town Hall

Completed in 1863, the Town Hall on King William St., Adelaide's main street, immediately captures the eye with its 44 m high tower which houses a set of bells installed in honour of Prince Albert. Inside the building, visitors can admire displays with memorabilia of Queen Adelaide, the consort of King William IV. of England. *Information: Tel: 08/82 18 72 11*

MUSEUMS

There are various museums in Adelaide, including a museum on immigration in South Australia

In Barossa Valley, 36 wineries invite you to sample their vines

(82 Kintore Av., Mon–Fri 10 am–5 pm, Sat, Sun 1–5 pm, Tel: 08/82 23 87 48), a museum on the maritime history of the state *(Lipson St. in Port Adelaide, Sat–Wed 10 am–5 pm, open daily during school holidays, Tel: 08/82 40 02 00)*, a postal museum *(2 Franklin St., Mon–Fri 11 am–2 pm, Tel: 08/82 16 22 25)* where letters are stamped with a special commemorative stamp, and a very interesting telecommunications museum *(131 King William St., Mon–Fri 10.30 am–3.30 pm, Sat 10.30–4 pm, Tel: 08/82 30 66 01)*.

Art Gallery of South Australia
The state gallery of paintings focuses on contemporary art but also has a remarkable collection of 17th century landscape paintings. *10 am–5 pm daily, North Tce., Tel: 08/82 23 72 00*

Old Parliament House
The former Parliament building now houses a Constitutional Museum – a political museum which features, among other displays, a 90 minute slide show on the history of Adelaide. *Mon–Fri 10 am–5 pm, Sat, Sun 12 am–5 pm, corner of North Tce./King Williams St., Tel: 08/82 12 68 81*

South Australia Museum
This museum boasts one of the largest collections of Aboriginal culture in the world. *10 am–5 pm daily, Wed from midday, free guided tours Sun 2.15 and 3 pm, North Tce., Tel: 08/82 23 89 11*

RESTAURANTS

Chloe's
This old, traditional restaurant is located in a stately mansion in

90

the suburb of Kent Town and offers very good French cuisine. *36 College Rd., Tel: 08/83 62 25 74, Category 2*

National Fish Cafe

Simple but good seafood restaurant near the pier in the resort suburb of Glenelg. Often crowded, reasonable prices. *30 Jetty Rd., Tel: 08/82 95 43 78, Category 3*

Rundle Street

★ Lively restaurant area with many street cafés and bars. Most of the restaurants serve Mediterranean food, others specialize in popular Australian-Asian cuisine. The most popular meeting place is the *Universal Wine Bar, 285 Rundle St., Tel: 08/82 32 50 00.*

HOTELS

Hyatt Regency

A luxury hotel in a very good location just a few short steps away from the Rundle Mall. *367 rooms, North Tce., Adelaide, WA 5000, Tel: 08/82 31 12 34, Fax: 82 31 11 20, Category 1*

The Mansion Apartments

Modern, well-furnished apartments behind a historic façade. Central location, all apartments equipped with kitchenettes – perfect for self-catering. *52 rooms, 21 Pulteney St., Adelaide, WA 5000, Tel: 08/82 23 45 59, Fax: 82 23 45 59, Category 2*

Moore's Brecknock Hotel

This is a small, simple hotel in a favourable location near the city centre. *8 rooms, 401 King William St., Adelaide South, WA 5000, Tel: 08/82 31 54 67, Fax: 84 10 19 68, Category 3*

ENTERTAINMENT

The "young and beautiful" of Adelaide like to spend their evenings in the *Old Lion Hotel,* a pub that brews its own beer and often has live bands on stage. Other popular meeting places to be found in this old hotel, include a discotheque and a restaurant. *163 Melbourne St., Tel: 08/82 67 37 66*

INFORMATION

South Australian Government Travel Centre

18 King William St., Adelaide, WA 5000, Tel: 08/82 12 15 05

SURROUNDING AREA

Barossa Valley   (164/C 5)

It was in this wide valley, some 50 km northeast of Adelaide, that a colony of Lutherans from Germany first settled in 1842 and started to make wine – marking the beginning of what has become a flourishing industry in Australia today. A total of 36 vineyards are available for wine tastings, and numerous restaurants offer regional wines as well as authentic German cuisine. The main town of the area is *Tanunda.* The biennial wine festival (odd years) begins on Easter Monday and, like the *Oktoberfest,* attracts visitors from all over Australia.

Kangaroo Island   (164/B 4)

★ This third largest island of Australia is 145 km long, and close to 20 per cent of its area has been turned into a reserve. The crossing to Cape Jervis, 110 km south of Adelaide, takes about an hour. *For departure times contact the SA Travel Centre .* There are also regu-

At Kangaroo Island you share the beach with sea lions

lar flights to and from the island in light aircraft. Seal Bay in the south of the island is the home of a colony of several hundred sea lions. You can even walk amoung them on the beach.

CEDUNA/ EYRE PENINSULA

The small town of Ceduna (pop. 4,000) marks the end of the deserted part of the southern route and the beginning of the vast wheat fields. Almost every town in this region is dominated by the huge grain silos. Near Ceduna is a fork in the highway, where Eyre Highway crosses the Eyre peninsula and heads for the ocean, reaching Port Augusta after some 486 km. Flinders Highway – later called Lincoln Highway – follows the coastline of the peninsula and then runs north to reach Port Augusta after 763 km. It will take you to a dramatic coastline as well as to fertile farmlands and finally min-

ing and industrial centres – a worthwhile detour if you have the time.

Ceduna (163/E 4)

The much-photographed signpost on main street has become the symbol of Ceduna. The *Old Schoolhouse National Trust Museum* shows relics from the British nuclear tests carried out in the South Australian desert near Maralinga *(Mon, Tue and Thu–Sat 10–midday and Wed 2–4 pm, Park Tce., Tel: 08/86 25 22 10).* Some 40 km northwest of Ceduna is the *Overseas Telecommunications Earth Station,* one of the main relay stations for the satellites over the Indian Ocean. *The station is open to visitors Monday to Friday. On most days, you can choose between two guided tours which begin at varying times of the day. For detailed information call Tel: 08/86 25 25 05, or contact the Gateway Tourist Information Centre, 46 Poynton St., Ceduna, SA 5690, Tel: 08/86 25 27 80, Mon–Fri 9 am–5.30 pm, Sat 9 am– 2 pm*

Eyre Peninsula (**163–164/E–B 4**)
Flinders Highway runs south past Smoky Bay to the fishing and resort town of *Streaky Bay* (**163/E 4**), some 112 km away. From there it is another 55 km to the south until you reach *Point Labatt* with its viewing platform from where you can watch, through a telescope, the only permanent colony of sea lions on the Australian mainland. When you take the unpaved road back to the Highway, you should stop at *Murphy's Haystacks.* These rocks, which from a distance look like haystacks, are 15 million year-old granite formations shaped by the wind and rain. There are several such formations on the peninsula.

The second largest city, *Port Lincoln* (**164/A 5**, pop. 13,000), lies on the east coast on the edge of Lincoln National Park, not far from the tip of the peninsula. The countless islands in Boston Bay are a wonderful sight. Further out at sea, at Dangerous Reef, more white sharks lurk in the water than anywhere else in the world. Several companies offer boat excursions out to these most dangerous of all fish. And if you are truly daring, you can don a diver's suit and let yourself be lowered into the water to be lowered into the water amongst the sharks. These tours are not cheap, and there is of course no guarantee that you will actually see a white shark. Port Lincoln runs a rather inefficient tourist information office from a travel bureau, so if you need help, it is probably better to turn to the *Eyre Peninsula Tourism Association (P.O. Box 1145, Port Lincoln, SA 5606, Tel: 08/ 86 82 46 88)* which will provide information on the entire penin-

sula. Heading north from Port Lincoln, Lincoln Highway, now called *Alt 1* (an alternative route to Highway 1) takes you to several seaside resorts before turning inland beyond Cowell and crossing the Middleback Ranges, where iron ore is mined. The best known mine is *Iron Knob* (**164/B 4**) which offers guided tours on weekday. From here the ore is transported to *Whyalla* (**164/B 4**) on the coast where it is processed in a huge steel mill *(guided tours available Mon, Wed, Sat at 9.30 am).* Visitors are required to wear special clothing. *For details contact the Tourist Information Centre (Lincoln Hwy., Whyalla, SA 5600, Tel: 08/86 45 79 00, Mon–Fri 8.45 am– 5.10 pm, Sat 9 am–4 pm, Sun and holidays 10 am–4 pm).* This information centre is located right next to the local *Maritime Museum (opening times: 10 am–4 pm daily, Tel: 08/86 45 89 00).* The main attraction of this interesting museum should not be missed: it is the former navy corvette "Whyalla" – the largest ship on land in the whole of Australia.

EUCLA/ EYRE HIGHWAY

(**162/C 4**) Close to the border between Western Australia and South Australia, 1,435 km from Perth and 1,236 km from Adelaide, is Eucla. This tiny village has only a handful of inhabitants but it is one of the few spots on the *Great Australian Bight* where you have access to the sea. Elsewhere, the coastline of this huge bay is dominated by rugged cliffs, battered by the surf of the ocean. It is no accident that the telegraph station, which enabled eastern Australia to communicate with the western half of the country for the first time, was built near Eucla in 1877 – it was not only possible for boats to land here, there was also a good supply of fresh water. Eucla also boasts one of the best-run motels along the transcontinental highway.

SIGHTS

Eucla National Park (162/C 4)
This small park (3,3 hectares) on the coast is only a ten minute drive from Eucla. This is where the steep limestone cliffs begin which continue westward for over 300 km – making it the longest uninterrupted stretch of cliffs in the world. From up high you can sometimes see whales, dolphins and sea lions off shore.

Eyre Highway (161–164/F–B 4)
Slightly longer than 1,200 km, this highway runs through one of the driest and most deserted parts of Australia. It traverses the *Nullarbor Plains* near its halfway point. The name "Nullarbor" is Latin and means "no trees" and in fact there is a 200 km stretch of road on which there are only a very few low bushes. The little rain that does fall drains immediately into the limestone where the water has carved out numerous caverns which are almost inaccessible and quite dangerous for the uninitiated. Also on this Highway is Australia's longest straight section of asphalt road – a 146.6 km long stretch east of Balladonia Station. Several side roads lead from the Highway to the edge of the 100 m high cliffs which are dangerous due to the porous rock. Roadhouses along the Highway are up to 200 km apart, so make sure that you always carry enough fuel and a sufficient quantity of water.

Telegraph Station (162/C 4)
★ Sand dunes have almost completely covered the telegraph station by now, but some of the walls are still visible. This was once the remotest telegraph station in the world, but also one of the busiest: Telegrams in Morse code from Western Australia were translated here by Western Australian operators and passed across the table to their South Australian colleagues who translated the words back into Morse code and sent them on. But it was not technical progress which eventually forced the station to close – it was the sand.

HOTEL

Eucla Motor Hotel
This well-managed complex combines a motel and roadhouse and can even boast a small garden – an unusual sight in this part of the desert. Some of the rooms enjoy a fine view of the sea, and the restaurant serves very tasty dishes. The owner of the hotel has set up a small museum in honour of John Eyre, the first man to successfully negotiate the east-west route (1841), and other pioneers. Not far from the hotel there is also a small stone monument honouring Eyre. And a few steps further on, there is a huge cross, illuminated at night, reaching up to the sky: "The Traveller's Cross." *23 rooms, on Eyre Highway, Tel: 08/90 39 34 68, Category 2–3*

PORT AUGUSTA

(164/B4) Port Augusta may not be known outside the country, but it is the most important road and rail junction in South Australia. It is here that Eyre Highway, running from east to west, crosses the Stuart Highway, the north-south link connecting Darwin and Adelaide. Port Augusta is also the junction of the transcontinental railway lines with the track going up to Alice Springs in the Red Centre. For a long time, however, this port situated at the northern tip of the Spencer Gulf (pop. 16,000) was more or less ignored. It was only when the town began to call attention to its old buildings and also established an Outback Centre (see below) that tourists began to come.

SIGHTS

Arid Lands Botanic Garden

This 200 hectare park on the northern edge of town presents a good collection of desert plants. The botanic garden, which is still in its first stages, also cultivates rare and endangered plants from the interior. There is an info centre and a bistro. *9 am–5 pm daily, Stuart Hwy., Tel: 08/86 41 10 49*

Homestead Park Pioneer Museum

This 130 year old farmhouse was dismantled on its old site and faithfully reassembled in the park. It has been furnished in period style. *10 am–5 pm daily, Elsie St., Tel: 08/86 42 20 35*

Royal Flying Doctor Service Base

Like most of the stations of this unique emergency service (RFDS) in the Outback, this base of the "Flying Doctors" in Port Augusta is also open to the public (guided tours only). *Mon–Fri 10 am–midday and 1–3 pm, 4 Vincent St., Tel: 08/ 86 42 20 44*

School of the Air

Like those of the "Flying Doctors" the bases of the "School of the Air" are also open to visitors. The school broadcasts lessons over the air to students on Outback stations and uses the communications network of the RFDS. *Open Mon–Fri 10 am, 59 Power Cr., Augusta Park Primary School, Tel: 08/86 42 20 77*

Wadlata Outback Centre

★ A modern wing, designed in the style of "Outback architecture", was added to this former 19th century convent to create an interesting blend of styles. The complex houses not only the Wadlata Outback Centre but also a small restaurant and the local Tourist Information Centre. The Outback Centre provides a good introduction to the geographical peculiarities of the Australian interior and its development as well as the way of life of the Aborigines. *Mon–Fri 9 am–5.30 pm, Sat 10 am–4 pm, 41 Flinders Tce., Port Augusta, SA 5700, Tel: 08/ 86 42 45 11 (Wadlata), Tel: 08/ 86 41 07 39 (Tourist Information)*

ACCOMMODATION

Hi-way One Motel

As the name indicates, this motel is located on Highway 1 south of the town in the direction of Adelaide. *44 rooms, all furnished in different styles, are available at varying rates, Tel: 08/86 42 27 55, Fax: 86 41 05 88*

Where the majority of Australians live

Melbourne: Victorian elegance in a great metropolis;
Canberra: Bustling capital from the drawing board

The south-eastern corner of Australia is one of the most densely populated regions on the fifth continent. At the heart of the region, on the shores of the vast Phillip Bay, is Melbourne, the country's second-largest city. Back in the 19th century, this financial centre had entertained hopes of becoming Australia's capital, but Sydney was a strong challenger and could claim seniority. By way of compromise, the nation's founding fathers decided to build a new capital – Canberra – further inland, placing it halfway between the two great rivals, Melbourne and Sydney. This chapter begins in Melbourne and takes you through the state of Victoria to Canberra which is given a special section.

MELBOURNE

☛ **City Map inside back cover**

(**168/C2**) The capital of Victoria is considered not just the "most British" of all Australian cities but also the "most European". The

The skyline of Melbourne makes for an impressive sight

former is, of course, owed to its "British attitude", the latter to the large number of Italian and Greek immigrants. Melbourne ranks as the second-largest "Greek" city in the world. The Victorian elegance of the architecture, the street cafés, the trams (a landmark of the city), the park, the wide variety of cultural offerings and the diversity of cuisines have all contributed to the distinctly European atmosphere in this city of three million.

SIGHTS

Australian Gallery of Sport & Olympic Museum

This museum is dedicated to ten different sports, including Australian rules football, a variety of rugby, which originated here in Melbourne, and tennis – the first grand slam tournament is played in the National Tennis Centre in January of every year. The Olympic Museum obviously focuses on the 1956 Summer Games in Melbourne, the first games to be held in Australia. Currently the collection is being enlarged for the 2000 Olympics in Sydney. *Next to the Melbourne Cricket*

97

MARCO POLO SELECTION: THE SOUTH-EAST

1 **National Gallery of Victoria**
The largest glass roof in the world, designed by Leonard French, is best appreciated by looking up from the floor
(page 99)

2 **Colonial Tramcar Restaurant**
This old tram is luxuriously furnished like a Victorian drawing room. Inside, you can dine like royalty, right in the centre of Melbourne
(page 101)

3 **A flight over the Shipwreck Coast**
The rock formations of the Twelve Apostles off the spectacular coastline are best seen from the air
(page 105)

4 **Parliament House**
Canberra's Parliament is one of the few in the world where constituents can get on top of their representatives by climbing on to the panted roof (page 108)

Ground (MCG) in Yarra Park, 10 am–4 pm daily, Tel: 03/96 54 89 22, tickets include a tour of the MCG; the Tennis Centre is accessible April–Sept only. Information: Tel: 03/96 55 12 34

City Centre

The main thoroughfare of this banking centre is *Swanston Street* (partly turned into a pedestrian zone) – bustling with activity. By contrast, *Flinders Street Station* at the end of Swanston Street is much more elegant. It is here that the thoroughfare crosses the Princess Bridge over the Yarra River which runs through Melbourne. Swanston Street is crossed by two important shopping streets: *Bourke Street* (partly pedestrianized) and *Collins Street* which is considered the top address in the city.

Cook's Cottage

The house in which James Cook's parents lived now stands in Fitzroy Gardens, a wonderful 150 year old park near the Parliament building. The house was dismantled at its original location in England and shipped to Australia in 1935 for the centenary of Melbourne. *The cottage is open to visitors 9 am–5 pm daily (Tel: 03/94 19 87 42).*

La Trobe's Cottage, King's Domain

Like so many other sights in Melbourne, the house of the first governor of Victoria is set in a park. It was brought over from England in 1839 and reassembled. When it fell into disrepair, it was restored and moved to King's Domain *(varying opening times, Tel: 03/96 54 45 62).* Other attractions in this neatly kept 40 hectare park on the south bank of the Yarra River are *Government House,* the *Shrine of Remembrance* (a War Memorial which boasts a rooftop balcony with a fine view of the city, *10 am–5 pm daily),* the *Myer Music Bowl* – a popular venue for open-air concerts – and the *Royal Botanical Gardens.*

Old Melbourne Goal

Built in 1841, this jail remained in use until 1929. Exhibits include the iron mask of Ned Kelly, the legendary bandit who was executed here. Kelly was the most popular of the "bushrangers" and is widely regarded as a folk hero today. *9.30 am–4.30 pm daily, Russell St., Tel: 03/96 63 72 28*

Parliament House

The Parliament of Victoria convenes in a stately building (erected 1856–92) at the upper end of Bourke and Collins Street. *Guided tours are available Mon–Fri at 10 and 11 am, 2, 3 and 3.45 pm, except during sessions of Parliament (Tel: 03/96 51 85 68).*

Royal Exhibition Building

Just north of Parliament House a palatial exhibition building with a 60 m high dome was erected in 1880 in Carlton Gardens for the Royal Exhibition. Designed by David Mitchell, the father of opera singer Nellie Melba, the building was used for the inaugural session of the Australian Parliament in 1901. To this day, the exhibition hall is still being used for trade fairs and various exhibitions.

Victorian Arts Centre

This Arts Centre is a modern complex on the south bank of the Yarra River at Princess Bridge. Its 115 m high steel structure has become a landmark of the city. The complex consists of several theatres, concert halls and exhibition facilities which are used for a variety of temporary exhibitions on themes related to the dramatic arts. *Call for programme information, Tel: 03/96 17 82 11*

MUSEUMS

Melbourne boasts more than a dozen museums, including a Chinese Museum in Chinatown *(Lonsdale St.),* a Fire Brigade Museum, a Railway Museum, an Aviation Museum as well as a Sports Museum and a Percy Grainger Museum in honour of the famous composer – to name just a few. The most famous is of course the National Gallery.

National Gallery of Victoria

★ This impressive collection of Australian artists and Aboriginal painters was given a new venue in 1968, right next to the Arts Centre. There are many works of the "Heidelberg School" which got its name from a suburb of Melbourne. The collection of Chinese art is also worth a visit. *10 am–5 pm daily, 180 St. Kilda Rd., Tel: 03/96 85 02 22*

National Museum of Victoria

A fascinating collection on natural history with numerous dioramas – quite old-fashioned and almost a museum piece in itself. The complex also includes a Museum of Science which has been especially designed for children and features a planetarium. This museum is scheduled to be moved to the Polly Woodside complex in the near future. *10 am–5 pm daily, 322 Swanston St., Tel: 03/96 69 99 97*

Polly Woodside

Somewhat outside the city centre, at the Spencer Street Bridge opposite the World Trade Centre, the "Polly Woodside" has found its final mooring in the Yarra River. The sailing ship, built in Belfast in 1885, is the centrepiece of the Maritime Museum. *10 am–4 pm daily, Sat, Sun to 5 pm, Tel: 03/96 99 97 60*

SHOPPING

Arcades and
Queen Victoria Market

Melbourne is Australia's fashion capital. The latest creations of the new fashion designers can be found in many places, e.g. in the *Southgate Center,* which houses not only shops and boutiques but also an aquarium. You should also explore the elegant arcades which look back on a long tradition – the *Royal Arcade* was opened in 1870. Other fine shopping areas include the tree-lined "Paris end" of *Collins Street* and the elegant suburb of *Toorak.* Less elegant but full of life is *Queen Victoria Market* which is more than 100 years old and covers some 6.5 hectares. This fascinating market offers a wide variety of products, from fresh vegetables to second-hand clothing *(Tue–Thu 6 am–2 pm, Fri to 6 pm, Sat to 1 pm, Sun 9 am–4 pm).* The most picturesque and comprehensive shopping complex is without a doubt *Melbourne Cen-*

Melbourne's elegant Royal Arcade looks back on a long tradition

100

tral, with its huge glass roof covering an old tower which has been listed as a historic monument (Swanston/Latrobe St., open on Sun as well). Of the numerous suburban markets, the best is probably the Sunday Art Bank in the seaside resort of St. Kilda on Phillip Bay. Every Sunday from 9 am to 6 pm, artists and craftsmen proudly display their latest creations on Upper Esplanade.

RESTAURANTS

Bistango

This small Versailles in miniature serves good food at reasonable prices. Lively atmosphere. Not far from the city centre. Discounts after 10 pm. Mon–Sat 5–12 pm, BYO, 470 Glenhuntly Rd., Elsternwick, Vic 3185, Tel: 03/ 95 23 05 00, Category 3

Champagne Charlie's

In spite of its "expensive" name and its location in the equally expensive surburb of Toorak, the prices are moderate. The food is well-prepared. With courtyard seating in the summer. 442 Toorak Rd., Toorak, Vic 3142, Tel: 03/ 98 27 59 36, Category 2

Colonial Tramcar Restaurant

★ Riding through the streets of Melbourne in an old tram, you can enjoy a full-course meal accompanied by a glass of wine. The point of departure is near the National Gallery. Tel: 03/ 96 96 40 00, Category 1–2

Stephanie's

Critics have been full of praise for Stephanie Alexander for years, although some of the culinary gloss seems to have worn off a bit lately. 405 Tooronga Rd., Hathorn East, Vic 3122, Tel: 03/98 22 89 44, Category 1

HOTELS

Flaggstaff City Motor Inn

A modern hotel near the Victoria Market. The hotel is especially popular with Australian businessmen on weekdays. 39 rooms, 45 Dudley St., Melbourne, Vic 3000, Tel: 03/93 29 57 88, Fax 93 29 85 59, Category 2

Grand Chancellor Hotel

Reasonably priced hotel in favourable location in the city centre. Ideal for visitors – all places of attraction are just a short walk away. 195 rooms, 131 Lonsdale St., Melbourne, Vic 3000, Tel: 03/96 63 31 61, Fax: 96 62 34 79, Category 2

Grand Hyatt Melbourne

Luxury hotel in one of Melbourne's best locations. The hotel features a heated swimming pool and various sports facilities including tennis courts. 577 rooms, 123 Collins St., Melbourne, Vic 3000, Tel: 03/96 57 12 34, Fax: 96 53 46 85, Category 1

Windor Hotel

Luxury hotel in a magnificently restored building next to Parliament, near the city centre. Listed by the National Trust. 190 rooms, Spring/Little Collins St., Melbourne, Vic 3000, Tel: 03/96 33 60 00, Fax: 96 33 60 01, Category 1

ENTERTAINMENT

Melbourne has a lot to offer in the evenings in terms of culture and entertainment. It is no longer like the 1970s, when visitors in-

Flinders Station is one of Melbourne's stateliest old buildings

quiring about night-life activities were advised to take the evening flight to Sydney. Things have changed for sure, and the formerly rather prudish city now offers everything you expect from a metropolis and a port city. There may be nothing that is particularly original, but try the areas with Italian restaurants, such as *Brunswick Street* in the Fitzroy district, or some of the traditional pubs. Two good examples are the *Botanical,* known as *Bot,* in the yuppie district of South Yarra *(169 Domain Rd., South Yarra, Vic 3141, Tel: 03/98 66 16 84)* and *Young and Jackson's* in the heart of the city centre *(Swanston/Flinders St., Melbourne, Vic 3000, Tel: 03/ 96 50 38 84).* Here, across the street from Flinders Street Station, you may experience some of the typical atmosphere of Aussie pubs. Upstairs you can admire Cloé, a nude painting that once caused a scandal in Melbourne.

INFORMATION

Victoria Visitor Information Centre
Swanston/Collins St., Town Hall, Melbourne, Vic 3001, Tel: 03/96 58 99 55, Fax: 96 53 97 33, Mon–Fri 8.30 am–5.30 pm, Sat, Sun 9 am–5 pm. The city has set up information booths in the pedestrian zone at Bourke Street and in Collins Street near City Square (Mon–Thu 9 am–5 pm, Fri to 7 pm, Sat 10 am–4 pm, Sun 11 am–4 pm).

SURROUNDING AREA

Geelong   (168/C 2)
This industrial town (pop. 130,000) about 75 km southwest of Melbourne is the home of the *National Wool Museum* which documents all aspects of this industry that has become a mainstay of the Australian economy. *Moorabool St., Geelong, Vic 3220, Tel: 03/52 26 46 00, 10 am–5 pm daily.* Good museum restaurant. The *Geelong Dive and Outdoor Centre*

(178 Moorabool St., Tel: 03/ 52 21 33 42) organizes all kinds of adventure tours including diving excursions to seal habitats.

Phillip Island   (168/C3)

This island, close to 130 km southeast of Melbourne, has been turned into a nature reserve with koalas, kangaroos, a seal colony and the "penguin parade". It is quite a spectacle every evening, when the returning fairy penguins gather on the beach before waddling home, past the stands crowded with visitors, to their nesting holes.

Queenscliff   (168/C2)

This little town at the entrance to Port Phillip Bay has become a favourite summer haunt for Melbourne's rich and famous. The old Victorian buildings, once the homes of sea pilots, have been lovingly restored. It was here at these narrows that in 1882 a fort was built to protect Melbourne from the perceived attacks of the Russian Navy which never came. The fort is now a museum. The old train station houses a railway museum. During the holidays and on weekends you can take a ride on an old train.

Torquay   (168/C2)

Thanks to its magnificent surf, this sea resort 20 km south of Geelong has become the centre of Australian surfing. *Surfworld Australia (Surfcoast Plaza, Beach Rd., Torquay, Vic 3228, Tel: 03/52 61 46 06)* boasts the country's largest exhibition on the subject of surfing. At *Torquay Airpark (Blackgate Rd., Tel: 03/52 61 51 00)* visitors can take a ride in one of the old biplanes.

ECHUCA

(168/C1) In the language of the Aborigines, the name of this town (pop. 9,500) means "where the waters meet." This is where two smaller rivers flow into the Murray River, the largest river in Australia. Until 1890, during the era of paddle steamers, Echuca was the busiest inland port in Australia. Today the town depends largely on the tourist trade, and there are only pleasure boats plying up and down the river.

SIGHTS

Njernda Aboriginal Cultural Centre

This museum documents the way of life and the art of the Australian Aborigines. The museum shop sells Aboriginal arts and crafts. *In the old courthouse on Law Place, Tue–Sun 10 am–4 pm, Tel: 03/54 82 39 04*

Port of Echuca

The old port with its wharf and two historic buildings has been carefully restored. One ticket grants you access to the entire complex – including the escape tunnels in the *Star Hotel* used by the moonshiners when police came to search the premises. *45 Murray Esplanade, 9 am–5 pm daily, Tel: 03/54 82 42 48.* Other attractions at the old port are the nearby *Red Gum Works,* a historic *saw mill (Murray Esplanade, 9 am–5 pm daily, Tel: 03/54 82 57 11),* the *Coach House* with its collection of old coaches *(37 Murray Esplanade, 9.30 am–3 pm daily, Tel: 03/ 54 82 52 44)* and *Sharp's Magic Movie House* with its lovingly restored vintage penny-arcade machines and a small cinema screening old films *(Murray Esplanade, 9 am–5 pm daily, Tel: 03/5482 23 61).*

World in Wax

Close to 70 wax figures, from the Pope to Paul Hogan, the hero of "Crocodile Dundee" are assembled in this wax museum. *630 High St., 9 am–5 pm daily, Tel: 03/ 5482 36 30*

Bridge Hotel

This pub, dating back to the year 1858, now forms part of the Old Harbour complex. The building houses a small museum, a good restaurant, a bistro and a beer garden. *Hopwood Pl., Echuca, Vic 3564, Tel: 03/5482 22 47, Category 2–3*

Steampacket Inn

Period hotel on the historic riverfront, now a listed building. *10 rooms, Lesley St./Murray Esplanade, Echuca, Vic 3564, Tel: 03/5482 34 11, Fax: 5482 64 13, Category 3*

Echuca and District Tourism Assocation

2 Leslie St. (old custom house), Echuca, Vic 3564, Tel: 03/5480 75 55, Fax: 5482 64 13, Mon–Fri 9 am–5 pm daily, Sat, Sun 10 am–4 pm

GREAT OCEAN ROAD

(168/B–C 2–3) This stretch of the coastal highway is almost 300 km long and one of the most spectacular routes in Australia. It is little known among visitors from abroad, with the possible exception perhaps of one of its scenic highlights, the "Twelve Apostles" in Port Campbell National Park. It is no coincidence that this area bears the name "shipwreck coast" – there are more than 30 ships on the floor of the sea. One of them was the "Loch Ard" from Scotland

Of the "Twelve Apostles" in Port Campbell National Park on Great Ocean Road, only ten are still left standing today

which sank in 1878 – one of the most beautiful bays on the coast was named after it. The coastal route between Geelong to the east and Mount Gambier to the west is 550 km long, and the Great Ocean Road is a part of this route. It begins at the resort of Torquay south of Geelong and ends in Warrnambool. The road was build in 1932 in an effort to provide work for the unemployed during the time of the Great Depression.

SIGHTS

Apollo Bay (168/C3)
This resort has two small museums. The *Old Cable Station Museum,* now a museum of local history, was originally the beginning of the first underwater cable from the Australian mainland to Tasmania. *Great Ocean Road, 15 km east of the town, Sat–Sun 2–4 pm, open daily during school holidays.* The *Bass Strait Shell Museum (12 Noel St., Apollo Bay, Vic 3233, 9.30 am–8 pm daily)* displays not only a collection of sea shells but also many other exhibits dealing with life on the coast. It is not far from here to *Otway National Park* and the old lighthouse of 1848.

Lorne (168/C3)
This traditional seaside resort at the mouth of the Erskine River is very popular with Australian families. ↘↗ *Teddy's Lookout* above the town provides a good view along the fascinating coast. Angahook Lorne State Park has a number of hiking trails. *Lorne Tourist Information Centre, 144 Mountjoy Parade, Lorne, Vic 3232, 8.30 am–4 pm daily, Tel: 03/ 52 89 11 52*

Port Campbell National Park (168/B3)
Of the "Twelve Apostles" a group of rock columns shaped by the forces of erosion off the steep cliffs, only ten have survived. There is no vista point on the entire coast from which you can see all ten "Apostles" – you need a trip on a sightseeing plane for that. Other impressive rock formations on the coast include *The Arch, London Bridge* (partly collapsed since 1990) and *Loch Ard Gorge* on the Shipwreck Coast, a bay to which you can climb down.

Sightseeing flights
★ ↘↗ The coast near Port Campbell National Park is best seen from the air. Several companies offer sightseeing flights; the oldest is *Shipwreck Coast Scenic Flights (departures from the Petersborough Airstrip, Vic 3270, Tel: 03/55 98 63 69).* Alternatively, you can also see the Twelve Apostels from a helicopter; for instance by companies such as *Helicopter Operators, 136 Bromfield St., Warrnambool, Vic 3280, Tel: 03/55 62 72 15*

Warrnambool (168/B2)
The main attraction of this town is the *Flagstaff Hill Maritime Village,* a reconstruction of a Victorian port with buildings and ships dating from that period *(Merri St., Warrnambool, Vic 3280, 9 am–5 pm daily, Tel: 03/55 64 78 41).* The *Tourist Information Centre (600 Raglan Parade, Warrnambool, Vic 3280, Tel: 03/55 64 78 37) is open 9 am– 5 pm daily.*

HOTELS

The hotels and motels on this most picturesque stretch of the

Great Ocean Road have set up a joint Shipwreck Coast Booking Office which can be called free of charge throughout Australia. *Tel: 008/81 79 89*

VICTORIAN GOLDFIELDS

Ballarat (**168/C2**), once the centre of the gold rush in Victoria, has preserved some of its splendid houses, particularly in Lydiard Street. The city (pop. 70,000) is some 110 km from Melbourne. *Bendigo* (**168/C1**), another former gold rush city with a population of 70,000 today, lies 120 km to the north. A popular sightseeing route, the *Goldfields Tourist Route,* links both towns and other places where gold was discovered. The route has a total length of about 500 km.

SIGHTS

Ballarat/Eureka Stockade Memorial

This memorial commemorates the 1854 uprising of gold diggers against the state. The stockade was named after a pub called Heureka (which is Greek for "I have found it"). The short rebellion marked the first truly democratic event in Australia's history *(Eureka/Stawell St., Tel: 03/53 31 22 81).* At the Eureka Exhibition nearby (*602 Eureka St., 9 am–5 pm daily, Tel: 03/53 31 52 88*) you can learn all about the historic background. "Blood on the Southern Cross" is the title of a nightly sound and light spectacle also recalling the event. *Sovereign Hill Museum village (extra ticket required, varying times, Tel: 03/53 31 19 44).*

Ballarat/Sovereign Hill

This picturesque reconstruction of a gold diggers' settlement offers coach rides, actors costumed as policemen, saloon dancers and bank robbers, and an opportunity to pan for gold. The tunnelling is authentic – in the old days, gold was actually mined here. *Main Rd./Bradshaw St., 9.30 am–5 pm daily, Tel: 03/53 31 19 44, the price of the ticket includes a visit to the Gold Museum.*

Bendigo/Central Deborah Mine

A former gold mine with 17 different levels off a main shaft which reaches down to a depth of 422 m. There is a guided tour underground as well as tours through the processing facilities at ground level *(Golden Link, Violet St., 9 am–5 pm daily, Tel: 03/54 43 80 70).* In combination with a visit to the mine you can book a tour of the city on an old-style tram. There is a separate *Goldmining Museum (10–12 am and 2–4 pm daily, Tel: 03/54 43 53 48)* in Sailors Gully Rd.

Bendigo/Chinese Joss House

Many Chinese worked in the gold fields, and the temple at Finn St. *(10 am–4 pm daily, during high season to 5 pm, Tel: 03/54 42 16 85)* is evidence of their culture. Likewise the *Golden Dragon Museum (5 Bridge St., 9.30 am–5 pm daily, Tel: 03/54 41 50 44).*

ACCOMMODATION

Bendigo Haymarket Motor Inn

Mid-range motel with acceptable furnishings. Quiet location. *10 rooms, 5 McIvor Rd., Bendigo, Vic 3550, Tel: 03/54 41 56 54, Fax: 54 41 56 55, Category 2–3*

Sovereign Hill

Accommodation in a rebuilt military camp with well-furnished rooms. *38 rooms, Main Rd., Ballarat, Tel: 53 31 19 44, Category 2*

Sovereign Park Motor Inn

With indoor pool and sports complex. *38 rooms, 217 Main Rd., Ballarat, Vic 3350, Tel: 03/53 31 39 55, Fax: 53 33 40 66, Category 2*

INFORMATION

Ballarat Tourist Office

Sturt/Albert St., Mon–Fri 9.15 am–5 pm, Sat, Sun 10 am 1 pm, Tel: 03/53 32 26 94, Fax: 53 32 79 77

Bendigo & District Information

Charing Cross, Kangaruh Flat, 9 am–5 pm daily, Tel: 03/54 44 44 33, Fax: 54 44 44 47

CANBERRA

(166/B–C 6, 169/E–F 1) The Australian federal capital has its own mini-state, the Australian Capital Territory (ACT). Canberra was built on a green-field site and was laid out on the drawing board, as you can see by the arrangement of streets around artificial Lake Griffin. Founded in 1913, Canberra is gradually becoming less sterile. Most of the 250,000 inhabitants work either for the government or for Parliament. Other sources of income are the university and the tourist trade.

VIEWS OF THE CITY

Black Mountain

Canberra is surrounded by several hills with special view

The unusual architecture of Parliament House in Canberra

points. The highest point is the 195 m high Telecom tower with viewing platform and revolving restaurant on the 825 m summit of Black Mountain. *9 am–10 pm daily, Tel: 02/62 48 19 11*

SIGHTS

High Court and National Library
On the south shore of the lake, on King Edward Terrace, the old Parliament House is flanked by two buildings, the *Supreme Court* with its impressive architecture and the *National Library. The court building is open 10 am–4 pm daily (Tel: 02/62 70 68 11).* The library, which features a large collection on Australia and the Pacific, is open *Mon–Thu 9 am–10 pm and Fri–Sun 9 am–4.45 pm, guided tours for visitors are available Mon–Fri 11.45 am and 2.45 pm, Tel: 02/62 62 11 11*

Lake Burley Griffin
This large man-made lake in the city centre is mostly surrounded by parkland. Boats and cycles can be rented and there are several picnic sites. A huge jet of water 140 m high shoots up to the sky *10–12 am and 2–4 pm daily (in summer also in the evenings)* – it is a memorial to Captain Cook, along with a model of the globe on the shore. The bell-tower on Aspen Island was erected in 1963 to commemorate Canberra's 50th anniversary *(53 bells ring Wed at 12.45 am and Sun at 2.45 pm).*

National Botanic Gardens
These gardens on 50 hectares of parkland at the edge of the city *(Clunies Ross St.)* feature all types of Australian landscapes with typical plants, including an artificial rainforest. *9 am–5 pm daily, Info Centre 9.30 am–4.30 pm (inquire here for details on the times of the guided tours)*

Parliament House
★ The new Parliament building on Capital Hill was inaugurated in 1988 on the occasion of Australia's bicentennial celebrations. The impressive building was designed by Italian architect Romaldo Giurgola and cost close to 1.1 million A$. Thanks to the green roof which is open to the public, it fits nicely into the landscape, thus completing the plans of American architect Walter Burley Griffin, who designed Canberra with two centres and three main axes. The building can be visited as part of a guided tour. The old Parliament House below the new building is to be turned into a museum. *10 am–5 pm daily (except during sessions)*

Royal Australian Mint
In the state mint, visitors can observe how coins are actually minted. Also worth visiting is the small Money Museum. The mint is located on *Denison Street* in the district of *Deakin. Mon–Fri 9 am–4 pm (note that there may not be any minting on Fri), Sat, Sun (no minting at weekends!) 10 am–3 pm, Tel: 02/62 83 32 44*

MUSEUMS

Australian National Gallery
This collection of paintings in a new building on the south shore of the lake not far from the Supreme Court comprises over 70,000 works of art. *10 am–5 pm daily, Guided tours at 11.15 am, 1.15 and 2.15 pm, Tel: 02/62 71 24 11*

Australian War Memorial

This building in neo-Byzantine style contains a memorial to the Australian soldiers who died in action and a museum dedicated to the Australians who fought in the World Wars, in Korea and in Vietnam. *Anzac Parade, 9 am– 4.45 pm daily, Tel: 02/62 43 42 11*

National Science & Technology Centre

This newest museum in the capital features some 200 hands-on models demonstrating scientific and technological principles – a great experience for all those interested in science. *On the lakeshore between the National Museum and the Supreme Court, 9 am–5 pm daily, Tel: 02/62 70 28 93*

Fringe Benefits Brasserie

A pleasant bistro with a bright and friendly atmosphere, serving light, imaginative dishes. Popular with many politicians. *54 Marcus Clarke St., Tel: 02/62 47 40 42, Category 2*

Gundaroo Pub Restaurant

"Colonial meals" with country music and dancing, all at a flat rate. Designed mostly for tourists, but quite well done nonetheless. *Cork St., Gundaroo, ACT, Tel: 02/62 95 36 77, Category 2–3*

Downtown Spero's Motel

A well-furnished, mid-range motel in a favourable location near the city centre of Canberra. *65 rooms, 82 Northbourne Av., Canberra, ACT 2601, Tel: 02/62 49 13 88, Category 2*

Hyatt Hotel Canberra

The top hotel of the capital is situated near Parliament and the embassy quarter on the main axis linking the city with the government district. *268 rooms, Commonwealth Av., Yarralumla, ACT 2600, Tel: 02/62 70 12 34, Fax: 02/62 81 59 98, Category 1*

Canberra Tourist Bureau

Jolimont Centre, Northbourne Av., Canberra, ACT 2601, Tel: 02/ 62 49 60 66, Fax: 62 05 07 76

Snowy Mountains   (169/E–F 1)

It takes about 90 minutes to get from Canberra to Cooma, the "Gateway to the Snowy Mountains". One of the largest hydroelectric systems in the world has been built in this mountain range. Some of the installations are open to visitors.

A national park has been established all around the highest mountain, 2,230 m high Mount Kosciuszko. In the summer the mountains are ideal for hiking, in winter they offer the best skiing in Australia. *Information at the Visitors Centre, 119 Sharp St., Cooma, NSW 2630, Tel: 02/64 50 17 42*

Tidbinbilla Deep Space Tracking Station   (169/E 1)

This satellite tracking station about 40 km southwest of Canberra monitors satellites and records their signals. Visitors are welcome and can learn about the work of the station and space technology from models, films and photographs. *9 am–5 pm daily, Tel: 02/62 49 08 11*

In the fiery heart of the continent

Lack of water and an inaccessible terrain characterize the vast, deserted interior of the continent

Red Centre is the name Australians have given the desert-like interior of their continent. Apart from the almost permanently blue skies, the dominating colour is red, thanks to the iron-rich soil. Green is something of a rarity. Whatever plants are growing here, have adopted a greyish hue instead in response to the hot and arid steppe. It is only after the occasional heavy rainfall that this desert land suddenly comes to life, showing fresh green and colourful blossoms. This is the heart of the continent, where many visitors expect to find the "true" Australia, the authentic culture of the Aborigines. They can certainly find what they are looking for, but of course not in Alice Springs, around Ayers Rock or right by the side of the much-travelled Stuart Highway.

ALICE SPRINGS

(**155/E4**) Alice Springs is quite a large city by Australian standards (pop. 25,000) and lies almost exactly in the heart of the continent and hence in the centre of a huge desert. In this bleak geographic location the city enjoys the great advantage of having access to a good supply of water in the form of a natural spring. That is also why the engineers who laid the first cable across Australia, decided to establish a telegraph station here in 1872. It became the focal point for what is the city centre today and also for the cattle farmers in the surrounding area. Thanks to its modern airport, it has also become a popular tourist destination and a point of departure for tours into the interior. Tourism has dramatically altered the city in many ways, for better or for worse. On the one hand, comfortable new hotels and better restaurants have been established, but on the other hand, some of the spirit and atmosphere of the old Alice Springs has been lost forever.

VIEW OF THE CITY

Anzac Hill

✈ This small hill at the northern edge of town offers a wonderful view over Alice Springs and the

An impressive sight: the red rocks of Standley Chasm near Alice Springs

picturesque area all around. At the south end of town you can see the gap in the Macdonnell Ranges which seem to block the town from the outside world.

SIGHTS

Frontier Camel Farm

To the south of the gap in the MacDonnell Range, the Old South Road branches off from the Highway. It runs past a date plantation to a camel farm which also exports dromedaries to Arabia. Some of the animals were reared on the farm, others were captured in the Outback. The latter are descendants of those camels which were once brought to Australia as beasts of labour and later driven off into the desert. Visitors have an opportunity to ride a camel. Other attractions nearby include a small museum as well as angora goat and reptile farms. *9 am–5 pm daily, Ross Hwy., Tel: 08/89 53 04 44*

Royal Flying Doctor Base

★ The dispatch centre of the "Flying Doctors" is linked by radio with even the remotest farms in the Outback. In case of an illness, the doctors give advice over the air; in serious cases they fly out to see their patients. Various bases of the "Flying Doctor" Service are scattered across the entire Outback. The station in Alice is

MARCO POLO SELECTION: THE RED CENTRE

1 Ballooning over Alice

Not exactly cheap and also rather cramped, but certainly an unforgettable experience: a balloon ride at sunrise. Warm clothes are recommended as it can get quite cold up there (page 115)

2 Calling on the Flying Doctors

The flying doctors in the outback are famous the world over as heroes of an Australian TV series. Visiting them at their homebase lets you see what they do and how dramatic their activities can actually become (page 112)

3 Desert first hand

If you want to really experience Ayers Rock and the vicinity and not just look at the red rock, you should join a tour with the rangers. They also offer night-time excursions where you can learn all about the Southern Cross, the great symbol of Australia's flag (page 117)

4 Sleeping in a cave

To escape from the heat, many of the inhabitants of Coober Pedy live in cozy caves. If you want to see what it's like, try staying at one of the cool cave hotels (page 118)

A strong rain turns the steppe into a green meadowland

open daily for visitors *(Apr–Nov Mon–Sat 9 am–3.30 Sun 1–4 pm, guided tours every half hour), Stuart Tce., Tel: 08/89 52 11 29.*

School of the Air

Children in the Outback do not attend school, they are educated over the radio. The students regularly submit their work by post and are flown to Alice from time to time for examinations. The School of the Air is open to vistors *Mon–Fri 1.30–3.30 pm* (except during school holidays). *Head St., Tel: 08/89 51 68 00*

Telegraph station

The old telegraph station is 3 km north of town and easily reached by bicycle (rentals available). The station complex has been listed as a historical monument. The rangers offer guided tours of the installation. In the original Alice spring nearby you can take a refreshing dip. *9 am–9 pm, in winter (Apr–Sept) to 7 pm, Tel: 08/89 52 39 93*

MUSEUMS

Adelaide House Museum

This former hospital has been turned into a museum for John Flynn, the legendary founder of the "Flying Doctors". The John Flynn Memorial Church next door was also built in his honour. Only open *Mar–Nov Mon–Fri 10 am–4 pm, Sat 10–midday, Todd Mall, Tel: 08/89 52 18 56*

Alice Springs Desert Park

Opened in 1997, this park presents an insight into the fauna in the arid interior of the continent. *9 am–9 pm daily, Larapinta Dr., Tel: 08/89 51 87 88*

Araluen Arts Centre

This modern arts centre just outside the town was modelled on a traditional farmstead. It is a venue not just for exhibitions of all kinds but also for theatre and ballet performances as well as concerts. *Larapinta Dr., Tel: 08/89 52 50 22*

Ghan Preservation Transport Hall of Fame

A museum on the history of railway and lorry transportation in the Outback. *Noris Bell Av., 10 km south of Alice Springs, 9 am–5 pm daily, Tel: 08/89 55 50 47*

Spencer and Gillen Museum

The Spencer and Gillen Collection in Ford Plaza is devoted to the flora and fauna of the territory and to Aboriginal art. *Museum 9 am–5 pm daily, Ford Plaza Building, Todd Mall, Tel: 08/89 52 53 78*

Strehlow Research Centre

Anthropologist Theodor Strehlow spent a long time living amoung Aborigines and compiled a large collection of sacred artefacts. *10 am–5 pm daily, Larapinta Dr., Tel: 08/89 51 80 00*

Aviation Museum

The collection of the *Central Australian Aviation Museum* on the former airport documents many of the achievements of the "Flying Doctors" and aviation pioneers, and also shows the perils of flying in the desert *(Mon–Fri 9 am–4 pm Sat, Sun 10 am–2 pm, Memorial Dr., Tel: 08/89 52 10 01).*

RESTAURANTS

Ainslies Restaurant

This award-winning restaurant specializes in fish and other seafood which is flown in directly from the coast. *Stephens Rd., Tel: 08/89 52 61 00, Category 2*

Jolly Swagman

An inexpensive, simple restaurant which opens for breakfast as early as 5.30 am – perfect for all those who want to make an early start. *Todd Plaza, Todd Mall, Tel: 08/89 52 36 33, Category 3*

HOTELS

Rydges Plaza Alice Springs

This luxury hotel near the gambling casino has all the amenities, including a heated pool – after all, nights in the desert can be quite cold. *Barrett Dr., Alice Springs, NT 0870, Tel: 08/89 52 80 00, Fax: 89 52 38 22, e-mail: rhralice@rydges.com.au, Category 1*

Territory Inn

Good traditional motel near the Mall and the Todd River (which is dry most of the time). *107 rooms, 11 Leichardt Tce., Alice Springs NT 0870, Tel: 08/89 52 20 66, Fax: 89 52 78 29, Category 2*

ENTERTAINMENT

Bush Restaurants

Various companies organize dinner in the Outback. Prices vary, depending on your choice of a basic barbecue or full-course dinners. In many cases, a guitarist and singer will supply the entertainment. The package usually includes commentaries on the countryside and, after dark, on the starry skies above. *Details of dates and prices in the Tourist Bureau*

The Winery

In spite of its desert location, Alice Springs has a very good irrigated vineyard with a restaurant some 15 km outside the city. Every Tue, Thu, Sat and Sun, Ted Egan presents his Outback Show with songs and story-telling. *Petrick Rd., Tel: 08/89 55 51 33, Category 2*

INFORMATION

**Central Australian
Tourist Industry Association**
*Hartley St./Gregory Tce., Alice Springs,
NT 0870, Tel: 08/89 52 58 00, Fax:
89 53 02 95*

SURROUNDING AREA

Arltunga
Historical Reserve   (155/F4)

After the discovery of gold in the
desert in 1887, a new settlement
was established 103 km east of
Alice Springs. Only a few ruins are
left today, but there is a good information centre documenting
the history of the gold rush. Water
is available. *Tel: 08/89 51 82 11*

Balloon ride at sunrise

★ ☙ There are several balloon-
ists who offer early-morning
rides in their hot-air balloons, a
champagne breakfast included.
*For information contact Tel: 08/
89 52 87 23*

Hermannsburg   (155/E4)

This former Lutheran mission,
founded in 1877, is now an Abo-

Protection against insects

riginal settlement with roughly
400 inhabitants. It was made
famous by Albert Namatjira
who painted western-style water-
colours. The *Art Gallery* shows
works by Namatjira and some of
his followers. *For information
contact Tel: 08/89 56 74 11*

Kings Canyon   (155/D4)

It may be an exaggeration to call
this gorge "Australia's Grand
Canyon" but it is quite impressive
nevertheless. In the bright sun-
light, the 200 m sheer cliff walls
with their spectacular layering

Insects

Australia is notorious for its billions of blow flies (called *blowies*
for short). They may be rather harmless and relatively small, but
they can be quite a nuisance. In the extremely dry climate of the
interior, they are constantly looking for moisture which they tend
to find in the corners of your eyes and in your nostrils. Even if
you constantly wave your hands across your face – derisively
referred to as the 'great Austalian salute' – you cannot get rid
of these bothersome pests. For sensitive tourists, special insect nets
are recommended which are fastened to your sun-hat. Equally
irritating, and also quite aggressive, are the mosquitoes which
are encountered in humid regions (they do not transmit malaria).
To fend them off, you should try different repellent lotions or
sprays until you find one that works well with your skin.

take on uncounted shades of yellow. The climb up the cliff is somewhat difficult and requires good shoes. A comfortable hotel has been established near Kings Canyon which is some 320 km from Alice. *(Tel: 08/89 56 74 42, Fax: 89 56 74 10, Category 2).*

MacDonnell Ranges (155/D–E 4)

Alice Springs is surrounded by some fantastic natural scenery. There are several impressive gaps through the MacDonnell Ranges near Alice, for example *Simpson's Gap,* which is about 22 km west of Alice Springs. The most famous canyon is without a doubt *Standley Chasm,* which is just over twice as far. The passage is no more than 9 m wide, and the almost vertical walls are a towering 100 m high. *8.30 am–4.30 pm daily*

Mereenie Loop Road (155/D–E 4–5)

This circular road links Alice Springs with King's Canyon and Ayers Rock. It is only partly asphalted and hence not recommended for vehicles without four-wheel drive. As the route takes you into the territory of the Aborigines, you must obtain a *Mereenie Tour Pass* (A$ 2). This describes the route and tells you something about the culture of the Aborigines. Accommodation at Glen Helen and at King's Canyon. *Info office in Alice Springs*

AYERS ROCK

(155/D 5) Ayers Rock, rising abruptly out of the flat plain, measuring more than 3 km in length – is quite literally Australia's biggest tourist attraction. The rock is a sacred shrine of the Aborigines and part of a national park named Uluru, which is the name the Aborigines have given to the rock. It appears to change colour depending on the position of the sun. There is a magnificent view from its 348 m high top, but the climb is quite strenuous and, although not forbidden, is not encouraged by the Aborigines. A circular trail, 9 km long, runs all around the rock and past nume-

Ayers Rock, a sacred place of the Aborigines in Uluru National Park

rous caves, some of which are not accessible. The park rangers offer various tours and information programmes. *For more information, contact the Visitor Centre at Ayers Rock Resort.* This new resort was set up in 1984 at the edge of the national park, 18 km away from the rock. Designed to blend into the landscape, the project cost 150 million A$ and comprises several hotels, from luxury palaces to simple lodges and even a campsite. In the resort, the rangers of the national park service run an information centre. Be sure to take a look at the well-designed cultural centre of the Aborigines right next to the rock: it symbolizes two snakes.

RESTAURANT

Ayers Rock Resort
This holiday complex with hotels and shopping plaza boasts eight different restaurants, from *haute cuisine* to takeaway hamburgers. There is also a well-stocked supermarket for all those who prefer to cook their own meals.

HOTELS

Sails in the Desert
This luxury hotel, built around a huge swimming pool, is certainly quite an impressive sight. *230 rooms, Ayers Rock Resort, Ayers Rock, NT 0872, Tel: 08/93 60 90 99, Fax: 93 32 45 55, Category 1*

Spinifex Lodge
Simple guest rooms complete with small kitchen. Shared toilet and bath for every two rooms. *8 rooms, Ayers Rock Resort, Ayers Rock, NT 0872, Tel: 08/93 60 90 99, Fax: 93 32 45 55, Category 2*

SURROUNDING AREA

Olgas   (155/D 5)
Some 32 km from Ayers Rock you can see the Olgas emerging from the sandy ground – 36 round sandstone mounds which make a strange, spectacular sight. The Aborigines call this formation Katatjuta, which translates as "mountain of many heads". Many visitors consider the Olgas, criss-crossed with countless canyons and up to 546 m high, to be much more exciting than Ayers Rock. One of the most interesting hikes takes you through the *Valley of the Winds.* The excursion follows a 6 km circular trail, for which you should set aside at least two hours.

Tours
★ The rangers of the Northern Territory Conservation Commission offer several information programmes as well as guided tours, including a night-time "star talk" under the star-studded firmament. *Visitors Centre, Ayers Rock Resort*

COOBER PEDY

(164/A 1) The town of Coober Pedy was established in 1915 when opals were discovered in the desert. In the language of the Aborigines, the name means "holes dug in the ground by white men". The holes were dug in the search for precious stones. To escape from the stifling heat, many of the prospectors dug their dwellings into the rock as well. 90 per cent of all opals worldwide come from Coober Pedy (pop. 2,500), which attracts more and more tourists. Most of them choose to stay in one of the cave hotels which come in different price categories.

SIGHTS

Crocodile Harry's Underground Home
Crocodile Harry's real name is Arvida von Blumental. He is one of the town's best known characters. His cave dwelling is situated about 6 km from the town centre. *For exact visiting times contact the Tourist Information Centre*

Opal Fields Tour
Several different operators offer bus tours through the moon-like landscape of the opal mines. Usually visitors are not permitted to get off the bus, as the ground is full of dangerous holes. Included in the tours are visits to a private cave dwelling, an old opal mine and one of the cave churches. *For details contact the Tourist Information Centre in Hutchison St., which most people refer to as Main Street*

Umoona Mine and Museum
This opal mine in the centre of Coober Pedy was forced to shut down because the galleries dug into the ground were beginning to endanger the foundations of the houses. Today, the mine has become a tourist attraction. Souvenirs and opals are also sold in this complex. *Main St., 8 am–7.30 pm daily, guided tours available at varying times, Tel: 08/86 72 52 88*

RESTAURANT

Old Miner's Dugout Cafe
This café is actually a cave restaurant in the city centre, specializing in traditional recipes and kanga-

roo meat. *Main St., Tel: 08/86 72 55 41, Category 2–3*

ACCOMMODATION

Underground Motel
★ Inexpensive cave motel with friendly management. Rooms furnished with TV. Self-service breakfast. *8 rooms, Catacomb Rd., P.O. Box 375, Coober Pedy, SA 5723, Tel: 08/86 72 53 24, Category 2*

INFORMATION

Tourist Information Centre
St. Nicholas St./Hutchison St., Mon–Fri 9 am–5 pm, Sat 9–12 am, Sun 2–5 pm, Tel: 08/86 72 52 98, Fax: 86 72 56 99

SURROUNDING AREA

Mail Run Day Tour (164/A–B 1)
A circular tour with the postman from Coober Pedy to Oodnadatta and William Creek. His all-terrain van has a specially designed passenger cab. The tour takes about twelve hours *(departures every Mon and Thu)*. Passengers can stop off in either of the towns and rejoin another Mail Run at their convenience. *Details in the Coober Pedy Underground Bookshop, Tel: 08/86 72 55 58*

Woomera (164/B 3)
For reasons of secrecy, this small town (pop. 1,700) established in 1947 in conjunction with the missile base of the same name, remained inaccessible for many years. Today, only the missile testing site and the space observation centre of Nurrungar are off-limits. The *Heritage Centre Museum* features exhibits on the culture of the Aborigines as well as missiles

The Underground Motel in Coober Pedy offers a cool and shady refuge

and other items of space-age technology *(Mar–Nov 9.30 am–4.30 pm daily).* Accommodation in the region: *Roxby Downs Motor Inn, Richardson Pl., Roxby Downs, SA 5725, Tel: 08/86 71 03 11.* The town is some 370 km south of Coober Pedy and 175 km north of Port Augusta.

KATHERINE

(149/E3) This town with a population of almost 7,500 is an important junction in the Outback, where the roads to Western Australia and to Queensland branch off. The town has become a tourist centre thanks to the gorges of the Katherine River in the nearby national park. Several tour operators offer various organized tours into the surrounding area; some of the tours also have Aborigines as guides.

SIGHTS

Cutta Cutta Caves

The limestone caves are 25 km south of Katherine. During the dry season, rangers organize tours through the underground where you can see rare species of bats as well as occasional snakes. *From Mar to late Nov, daily tours available at 9, 10, 11 am and 1, 2, 3 pm*

Edith Falls

This waterfall feeds a lake which is very popular for swimming. All around the lake rich vegetation has developed. The lake is part of the *Katherine Gorge National Park,* even though it is actually quite a distance away from the gorges. There are additional pools, perfect for bathing, above the falls. Turn off Stuart Highway 40 km north of Katherine and follow the road for 20 km.

Katherine Gorge National Park

In the Aboriginal language, the park is called Nitmiluk. Its main attractions are a series of 13 successive gorges with a total length of 12 km. Depending on the water level, visitors can explore from two up to five of the gorges on organized boat tours. The only time of the year when it is possible to pass through all of the gorges is during the month of March. Throughout the Australian winter, several day-tours are available which are led by Aboriginal guides. *The information centre at the landing stage is open 9 am–4 pm daily*

Springvale Homestead

This farm is one of the oldest in the Northern Territory and has become a major tourist destination. Its main attractions include night excursions to the crocodile banks in the river and free guided tours of the farm. It is 8 km from Katherine and easily reached by following the Victoria Highway *Shadforth Rd., Katherine, NT 0850, Tel: 08/89 72 13 55*

Katherine Museum

This local history museum has found its home in the former terminal of Katherine's airport. The greatest showpiece of the permanent exhibition is a single-engine double-decker plane once used by Clyde Fenton, one of the first of the "Flying Doctors". *Gorge St., Mon–Fri 10 am–4 pm, Sat 10 am–2 pm, Sun 2–5 pm.* An additional museum has been established in the former railway station. It documents the history of the rail line from Adelaide to Darwin which has still not been completed.

Pine Tree Motel

Well-equipped motel in the centre of town. The pool is fringed with palm trees. *50 rooms, 3 Third St., Katherine NT 0850, Tel: 08/89 72 25 33, Fax: 89 72 29 20, e-mail: travelnorth@Pobox.com, Category 2*

Visitors Information Centre

Stuart Hwy./Lindsay Tce., Katherine, NT 0850, Mon–Fri 8.45 am–5 pm, Tel: 08/89 72 26 50, Fax: 89 72 29 69, e-mail: krta@nt-tech.com.au

Mataranka   (149/E 4)

Crystal-clear hot springs are the main attraction of Mataranka. Restaurant and motel provide bathing cabins free of charge. The homestead, which is actually an old Australian farmhouse, offers numerous sports and leisure facilities. The waterways all around Mataranka are teeming with Barramundis – these big fish are fed every day. The waterways cross over into the adjoining *Elsey National Park.* Canoes are available for hire in Mataranka. *110 km south of Katherine, Homestead Rd., Mataranka, NT 0852, Tel: 08/89 75 45 44*

TENNANT CREEK

(155/E 1) This small gold and copper mining town (pop. 3,400) is beginning to make a name for itself as a tourist destination by emphasizing not only the history of gold mining but also the way of life of the Aborigines. There are efforts to involve the native Australians in the community in order to combat the problem of alcoholism – a major problem which also faces other towns in the Outback. Tennant Creek is 961 km south of Darwin and 396 km north of Alice Springs.

SIGHTS

Dot Mine
Colonel Bremner, a veteran gold miner from the old days, takes visitors around his former mine. In the evening, they are invited to sit around the camp fire and listen to his stories.

Gold Stamp Battery
This old processing plant for gold ore has been restored and is put into action for the benefit of visitors. It is fascinating to watch the rocks being crushed by huge hammers. *Daily guided tours Apr–Oct 8 am and 5.15 pm.* From here it is not very far to the lookout point at *Nobles Nob Mine.* When it was still in operation, it was the largest open-cast gold mine in Australia.

MUSEUMS

National Trust Museum
Local history museum in a former field hospital built by the Army in 1942. *Apr–Oct 3.30–5.30 pm daily, for other opening times contact the Visitor Information Centre*

Overland Telegraph Station
This telegraph relay station of 1872 has been turned into a museum devoted to the cables which once joined Australia with the rest of the world. *Opening times vary; for details contact the Tennant Creek Visitor Information Centre*

RESTAURANT

Dolly Pot Inn
Lively bistro and pub with a beer garden and air-conditioned squash courts. *Davidson St., open daily for lunch and dinner, Tel: 08/89 62 28 24, Category 2–3*

ACCOMMODATION

Bluestone Motor Inn
Modern-style comfortable motel. The newer bungalows are more spacious than the old ones. *65 rooms, Paterson St., Tennant Creek, NT 0860, Tel: 08/89 62 26 17, Fax: 89 62 28 83, Category 2–3*

INFORMATION

Visitor Information Centre
Battery Hill Regional Centre, Peko Rd., Tennant Creek, NT 0860, Tel: 08/89 62 33 88, Fax: 89 62 25 09, e-mail: tcrta@topend.com.au

SURROUNDING AREA

Devil's Marbles   (155/E 2)
These curiously shaped rocks were formed over the millenia by wind, sand and the occasional rain shower. According to the mythology of the Aborigines these Devil's Marbles are eggs laid by the sacred Rainbow Serpent. *110 km south of Tennant Creek on Stuart Hwy.*

Moonlight Rockhole Fossicking Area   (155/E 1)
Some 53 km northwest of Tennant Creek you come to an abandoned gold mining area where anyone is welcome to look for nuggets. *All you need is a "Miners Right". Ask for details at the Visitor Information Centre*

An apple island in the south

It was in the homeland of the Tasmanian devil that Australian environmentalists won their first great victories

Tasmania, Australia's largest island some 330 km off the coast, is also its smallest state. The "Apple Island", named after its fruit exports, is a popular holiday destination for Australians. Relatively few foreign tourists ever make it to Tasmania. For one thing, the island lies somewhat off the beaten track (flights to Hobart, ferries from Melbourne and Sydney), for another, the Tasmanian landscape with forests and mountains may be something out of the ordinary for Australians but not for Europeans and Americans. It is a little known fact, however, that more than half of the island is still covered by virgin forests – it is the habitat of the Tasmanian devil, a carnivorous marsupial.

Tasmania may be the smallest state, but it can boast the largest national park in Australia – Cradle Mountain/Lake St. Clair with a total area of 135,000 hectares. In addition, it also has an extremely vigilant environmental organization. It was in Tasmania that the Green movement first started, and it is thanks to their efforts that ecological issues have been raised in other Australian states as well.

HOBART

(**169/D 6**) The first settlements on the island of *Van Diemen's Land,* which is what Tasmania was originally called, date from 1804 just a few years after the first shiploads of convicts landed at Sydney Cove. One of these early settlements was Hobart, now the capital of Tasmania. Thanks to the wool and whaling trades, the city prospered relatively quickly, and cheap convict labour facilitated the construction of several stately buildings which still embellish the city of Hobart (pop. 180,000) today. With the end of the convict era and the decline of the whaling industry, things began to quieten down in the Hobart region. Tasmania only made the headlines when the first legal gambling casino was opened here in 1973, or when a freighter collided with the 94 m high bridge across the Derwent River in 1975, causing

This church was part of the former convicts' colony in Port Arthur

123

parts of it to collapse, or when the Greens achieved their first great victory in the 1980s by preventing the construction of a reservoir in the Tasmanian forest.

Anglesea Barracks

The oldest barracks in Australia still in use date back to the years 1811–1828, although the two-storey buildings were erected later around 1850. *The complex in Davey St. is open to visitors 9 am–5 pm on weekdays; there is no public access to the buildings themselves, however. A guided tour is usually available every Tue at 11 am.*

Battery Point

Hobart's main tourist attractions are concentrated in the area around the harbour, away from

VIEW OF THE CITY

Mount Wellington

❧ It is about 20 km on the as-phalt road from Hobart to Mount Wellington. On a clear day, the view from its 1270 m high sum-mit encompasses not only the city and the mouth of the Derwent River but also the entire Tasman Peninsula and a large part of south-eastern Tasmania as well.

MARCO POLO SELECTION: TASMANIA

1 Harbour market
The Saturday market in Hobart on Salamanca Place (Battery Point) is still a popular meeting place for tourists and locals – and a great opportunity to hunt for some unsual bargain souvenirs (page 125)

2 New plays on an old stage
Tourists from abroad rarely make it to the Theatre Royal in Hobart. The playbill may not feature the greatest plays or the latest hits, but the atmosphere in this oldest theatre on the entire continent makes it worth visiting (page 127)

3 National Heritage shop
Now that umbrellas have become mass-produced items, they are no longer seen as a status symbol. This shop in Launceston, which has been taken over by the National Trust, recalls the heyday of umbrellas (page 130)

4 Lunar landscape created by man
In Tasmania, Australian environmentalists won their greatest victories, but it is also the site of one of the greatest crimes against Nature: What the lumberjacks did not cut down, perished in the sulphur vapours pouring forth from the smelters (page 129)

The port of Hobart is surrounded with historic sights

the city centre, and especially in the district of Battery Point, named after the battery of guns set up on this headland. According to historians, this ensemble of buildings dating from the early and mid-19th century is the best preserved example of its kind in all Australia. The narrow streets, the tightly packed houses, Arthur's Circus, one-time village green, and the ever-present atmosphere of the harbour still evoke a sense of what life must have been like for the first settlers in this region. The oldest surviving building, a signal station, dates back to the year 1818.

The most impressive buildings, however, are the old *warehouses* (1835–60) around *Salamanca Place,* which now house a variety of restaurants, galleries, boutiques and other shops. Every Saturday morning, a ★ ✪ market is held outside the warehouses (inside when the weather is bad). Guided tours around Battery Point are also offered at the same time.

Parliament House

This richly decorated building – originally a customs house – was built by convicts between 1835 and 1840. Tasmania's parliament has been meeting here since

1856. Guided tours are not available, but the public is given access to the visitor's gallery when parliament is in session. Next to Parliament House is *David's Park,* Hobart's first cemetery. Some of the graves bear the names of some of the early pioneers.

Royal Tasmanian Botanical Gardens

Some 2 km from the city centre, these botanical gardens, covering an area of 13.5 hectares, were once part of the neighbouring Government House. Perhaps the greatest attraction of the garden is the historic Arthur Wall with a heating system for exotic fruit and flowers. *8 am–4.45 pm daily (May–Aug), 8 am–5.30 pm (Apr, Sept–Oct), 8 am–4.30 pm (Nov–Mar), Lower Domain Rd., Tel: 03/ 62 34 62 99*

MUSEUMS

Maritime Museum

This museum in Secheron House, a building dating from 1831 in Battery Point, focuses on Tasmania's maritime history and on the whaling industry. *Sun–Fri 1–4.30 pm, Sat 10 am–4.30 pm, Secheron Rd., Tel: 03/62 23 50 82*

The Tasmanian Museum and Art Gallery

This museum complex in the city centre also includes the oldest building in Hobart, the *Commissariat Store* dating from 1808. The museum is devoted especially to the colonial history of the island and the fate of the Tasmanian Aborigines who were cruelly wiped out by the white settlers. *10 am–5 pm, 5 Argyle St., Tel: 03/62 23 14 22*

Van Diemen's Land Folk Museum

This wonderful museum on the history of the pioneer settlers on the island has been set up in *Narryna* manor at Battery Point. The elegant sandstone building in Georgian style was erected in 1833–36, and it has been furnished in period style. *Mon–Fri 10 am–5 pm and Sat, Sun 2–5 pm, closed in July, 103 Hampden Rd., Tel: 03/62 34 27 91*

RESTAURANTS

Beefeater

As the name suggests, meat dishes are the speciality of this restaurant which is housed in a building of 1850. Recommended is saddle of lamb. *37 Montpellier Retreat, Battery Point, Tas 7004, Tel: 03/ 62 23 87 00, Category 2–3*

Dear Friends

A converted windmill full of Victorian charm houses one of the best restaurants in Tasmania. Game is a speciality. *8 Brooke St., Hobart, Tas 7000, Tel: 03/62 23 26 46, Category 2*

HOTELS

Barton Cottage

A two-storey cottage in the historic town centre. The interior is well-equipped (all rooms with bath), the furnishings are in tasteful Colonial style. Bed and breakfast. *6 rooms, 72 Hampden Rd., Battery Point, Tas 7004, Tel: 03/ 62 24 16 06, Fax: 62 24 17 24, Category 2*

Grand Chancellor Hotel

✴✴ Situated right next to the historic docks, this luxury hotel offers a good view across the harbour and Battery Point. Heated indoor pool and a fitness gym. *234 rooms, 1 Davey St, Hobart Tas 7000, Tel: 03/62 35 45 35, Fax: 62 23 81 75, Category 1*

ENTERTAINMENT

Theatre Royal
★ The oldest theatre in Australia was built in 1837. Renovated some years ago, it is now a popular venue once again. *29 Campbell St., Tel: 03/62 34 62 66*

INFORMATION

Tasmanian
Travel and Information Centre
20 Davey St., Hobart, Tas 7000, Tel: 03/62 30 82 33, Fax: 62 24 02 89

SURROUNDING AREA

New Norfolk   (169/D 6)
Built in 1803, this little town (pop. 6,000) was once surrounded by fields of hops. In the historic *Oast House* you can learn all about hop growing – although the industry has lost some of its former relevance. The *Old Colonial Inn* has been turned into a local history museum, but the *Bush Inn* is still a working pub, which claims to have the oldest alcohol licence in Australia. Tasmania's oldest church, *St. Matthew's Church of England,* dates from about the same time.

Port Arthur   (169/D 6)
One of Tasmania's greatest attractions. Every year, more than 200,000 visitors come to see the impressive ruins of the old penal colony of Port Arthur. After being neglected for a long time, the historic complex has been re-

stored at a cost of about 9 million Australian dollars. Back in colonial times, Port Arthur was quite infamous. Between 1830 and 1877 no less than 12,500 convicts were imprisoned here, including some of the worst offenders and a number of children as well. The four-storey cell block was usually filled to capacity. Conditions were not quite as cruel as often alleged, as long as the inmates observed the prison rules. There were actually some (rather dubious) attempts at reforming the penal system, abolishing the previously widespread corporal punishment and replacing it with a calmer regime. The prison itself was considered quite safe, as the peninsula was guarded by watchdogs, barriers and a signalling system which extended all the way to Hobart. On top of that, the sea was teeming with sharks, so that few prisoners would consider swimming to freedom. "Ghost Tours" are offered every evening with uncanny tales by the light of a lantern. Port Arthur is 100 km from Hobart. *Daily tours every hour, beginning at 9.30 am, last tour at 3.30 pm, info Tel: 03/62 50 23 63*

Richmond   (169/D 6)
This historic little town, some 25 km away from the capital, is renowned for its Georgian town centre. Here you can find the oldest bridge in Australia (1823) as well as the oldest Catholic church. The courthouse is at least 170 years old.

DEVONPORT

(169/D 4–5) Devonport is an extremely busy port due to its proximity to the Australian mainland.

There is an old lighthouse dating from 1889 on Mersey Bluff which marks the mouth of the Mersey River. This is where the ferry from Melbourne docks. The "Spirit of Tasmania", which once served as a ferry in the Baltic, provides a regular night-time service across Bass Strait which separates the two places.

MUSEUMS

Don River Railway and Museum
This old-timer railway runs along the banks of the Don River (6 km west of town). The museum exhibits steam locomotives and railway cars of yesteryear. *Forth Main Rd., Don, Tas 7310, 11 am–4 pm daily, Tel: 03/64 24 63 35*

Tasmanian Maritime and Folk Museum
This museum, which is primarily devoted to the history of the harbour, prides itself on a great collection of models of early sailing ships. *47 Victoria Parade, Tue–Sun 2–5 pm, Tel: 03/64 24 71 00*

Tiagara
Numerous Aboriginal drawings were discovered on the cliffs of Mersey Bluff, making this an ideal place for Tiagara, the Tasmanian Aborigines Culture and Arts Centre. Exhibits trace the tragic history of the persecution and ultimate extinction of Tasmania's native population. *Mersey Bluff, 9 am–4 pm daily, Sept–May to 4.30 pm, Tel: 03/64 24 82 50*

RESTAURANT

The Old Rectory
This restaurant is fully licensed, but guests are equally welcome if they prefer to bring their own. *Murray/Wright St., Tel: 03/64 27 80 37, Category 2*

HOTEL

Riverview Lodge
Comfortable small guest house (11 rooms) in a good location on the Mersey. *11 rooms, 18 Victoria Parade, Devonport, Tas 7310, Tel & Fax: 03/64 24 73 57, Category 3*

Cataract Gorge is a popular place for picnicking and swimming

**Tasmanian Travel
and Information Centre**
*5 Best St., Devonport Showcase,
Devonport, Tas 7310, Tel: 03/
64 24 44 66, no Fax*

Burnie (168/C 4)
The main attraction of this industrial port on the north coast (pop. 21,000) is probably the *Pioneer Village Museum (High St., Mon–Fri 9 am–5 pm, Tel: 03/64 30 57 46)* with its historic reconstruction of an early street scene. Garden fans will enjoy the *Emu Valley Rhododendron Garden (via Mount Rd., Sept–Mar 10 am–5 pm daily, Tel: 03/64 33 02 55). For information, contact the Tasmanian Travel and Information Centre, 48 Cattley St., Burnie, Tas 7320, Tel: 03/64 34 61 22*

Great Circle Route
This 1000 km circular tour takes you from Devonport westward to Burnie, then south across the mountains to Queenstown, east to Hobart, along the east coast to Swansea and St. Helens, and then in a north-westerly direction back to Launceston and, finally, Devonport. You will not only see the untouched wilderness in the west but also the major cities and beaches in the east.

Queenstown (168/C 5)
★ This mining town in the mountainous interior is a perfect example of reckless exploitation: All the forests in the area were cut down for firewood for the mines, the remaining flora was destroyed by acid fumes from the smelters, and the resulting erosion has removed all soil from the bedrock. The landscape around Queenstown appears as barren as the moon – certainly an impressive though horrible sight. The history of the town (pop. 3,800) is documented in the *Galley Museum (Driffield/Sticht St., Mon–Fri 10–12.30 am, Sat, Sun 1.30–4.30 pm, closed in July)*

LAUNCESTON

(169/D 5) Launceston, Tasmania's second-largest city (pop. 85,000), also boasts the second-biggest (after Port Arthur) tourist attraction on the island: a spectacular gorge almost in the heart of the city. Northern Tasmania's commericial centre is also the third-oldest city in Australia: it was founded back in 1804 in this fertile valley. Correspondingly, the streets are lined with numerous historic buildings. Launceston lies on the upper reaches of the Tamar River which begins at the confluence of two smaller rivers. 65 km to the north, the wide Tamar River flows into the Bass Strait which separates Tasmania from the Australian mainland. The lively tourist trade prompted the gambling casino in Hobart to establish a similar one in the local country club.

Cataract Gorge
The South Esk River, which has created this steep gorge, widens out after passing through this gap and joins with the North Esk River to form the Tamar River. There is a hiking trail through the gorge up to the First Basin, a natural lake which is now

part of a almost 2 sq km nature reserve. On one side of the lake, rhododendron bushes and other plants proliferate; on the other side, the Cliff Grounds invite visitors to go for a swim or to have a picnic. Both banks are joined by an almost 460 m long chair-lift which affords a great view of the river and its banks. Higher up in the gorge itself you can see the remains of the former Duck Reach power station. When its turbines were set in motion in 1895, Launceston became the first city in the southern hemisphere to have electricity generated by water. The original turbine building was partly destroyed during a heavy flood in 1929. Admission to Cataract Gorge is free, but a charge is imposed for the chair-lift. In the evening, the gorge is illuminated although times vary according to the season.

Penny Royal World
This American-style combination of open-air museum and theme park is set in an abandoned quarry at the entrance to Cataract Gorge. Penny Royal World features a reconstructed windmill as well as a water-mill brought here from other regions of Tasmania. Also included in the complex are an old canon foundry and several ships which have been armed with cannons. Occasionally a demonstration gun-battle is staged. A restored tram transports visitors through the entire park. *9 am–5.30 pm daily, 147 Paterson St., Tel: 03/63 31 66 99*

Walking tour of the town
There are a number of historic buildings grouped around Civic Square, among them *Macquarie House,* which was built in 1830 as a warehouse and today houses a restaurant and the local history collection of the *Queen Victoria Museum.* From here it is only a few steps to the *Town Hall,* erected in 1864 in a mixture of Victorian and Italian architecture with an impressive columned façade. By contrast, the *Post Office* is a fine example of Queen Anne architecture. It was built in 1889, and the impressive tower was added in 1903. On the next city block, the *National Trust (60 George St.)* has its offices. It also runs a ★ souvenir shop which has been set up in an old umbrella store that has been preserved with all its furnishings – quite a unique and surprising attraction which definitely merits a closer look.

MUSEUMS

Community History Museum
The former Maritime Museum has expanded its collection to all fields of regional history. The exhibits are now housed in an old warehouse dating from about 1842. *Mon–Sat 10 am–4 pm, Sun 2–4 pm, St. John/Cimetière St., Tel: 03/63 37 13 90*

Queen Victoria Museum & Art Gallery
The art collection shown in this building from the last turn of the century, contains a number of impressive paintings from the early colonial period of Tasmania. The museum exhibits include artefacts from the now-extinct Aboriginal civilization, reminders of the also extinct Tasmanian tiger, a collection of objects from the convict camps and a Chinese joss

temple – a legacy from the descendants of Chinese immigrants. *Mon–Sat 10 am–5 pm, Sun 12 am–5 pm, Wellington St., Tel: 03/63 31 67 77*

RESTAURANTS

Quigleys
This French-inspired restaurant in an old building dating from 1860 also offers its guests Tasmanian wines. *96 Balfour St., Tel: 03/63 31 69 71, Category 1–2*

Shrimps
Specializing in fish and other sea food dishes. Seating in a glass-roofed courtyard. *Paterson/George St., Tel: 03/63 34 05 84, Category 2*

HOTELS

Hillview House
A well-maintained Bed & Breakfast in a 150 year old house. All the rooms are equipped with a private bathroom. *10 rooms, 193 George St., Launceston, Tas 7250, Tel and Fax: 03/63 31 73 88, Category 3*

Novotel Launceston
Central location. In the style of a traditional European grand hotel. *172 rooms, 29 Cameron St., Launceston, Tas 7250, Tel: 03/63 34 34 34, Fax: 63 31 73 47, Category 1*

INFORMATION

Tasmanian Travel Centre
Paterson/St. John St., Launceston, Tas 7250, Tel: 03/63 36 31 33, no Fax

SURROUNDING AREA

Evandale (169/D 5)
This community (pop. 850), some 20 km south of Launceston,

Launceston Town Hall was built in Victorian style

was founded in 1829. As it lies somewhat off the beaten track, it was able to preserve most of its original charm. The town as a whole has been officially listed as a historic monument by the Australian National Trust. The magnificent estate of *Clarendon (Tel: 03/63 98 62 20)*, situated 8 km outside Evandale, is set in a wonderful parkland area.

Ross (169/D 5)
This bridge across the Macquarie River is not just one of the oldest bridges in Australia but also one the most beautiful. It was built in 1836 with convict labour, and the stonemasons were rewarded for their efforts by granting them a pardon. The charming historic village (pop. 300) lies halfway between Launceston and Hobart. The *Tasmanian Wool Centre* documents the history of the fine wool spun in this region. *(Church St., Sept–Apr 9.30 am–5.30 pm daily, May–Aug 10 am–4 pm, Tel: 03/63 81 54 66)*

Travelling across the continent

These routes are marked in green on the map on the inside front cover and in the Road Atlas beginning on page 148

① TAKING THE TRAIN FROM COAST TO COAST

Australia is the only continent which you can cross by rail without having to change trains. The "Indian-Pacific" covers the 4,352 km from Perth to Sydney in 65 hours. The route is an absolute highlight and a must for all railway aficionados. At any rate, it is a comfortable way of seeing almost all the different landscapes Australia has to offer and to meet lots of people. Don't forget to book seats well in advance!

The Indian Ocean is no longer visible behind the highrise towers of *Perth (p. 73)*. A few minutes later, however, the train has left the suburbs of the Western Australian capital behind, and the long chain of shiny aluminium-clad cars behind the two powerful diesel locomotives winds its way through the mountainous landscape of the Darling Rangers like a silvery serpent. A group of wallabies can be seen jumping through the eucalyptus trees, apparently roused by the penetrating whistle of the locomotive.

The steward knocks and brings a cup of coffee. He writes down the requests of the passengers entrusted to his care. First or second dinner sitting? And at what time would you like your morning tea – or coffee – brought to your bedside? By now, the "express" has reached the plains, maintaining a steady, rather leisurely pace. The sun is setting dramatically beyond the steppe and the first small salt lakes – time for a "sundowner" in the first-class saloon car with its Victorian-style furnishings. And then the call to dinner in the restaurant car where the menu offers you a choice of three main courses and two desserts.

After dinner, there is plenty of time for a nightcap in the saloon – with a separate section reserved for smokers. Back in the compartment, the beds have been made and the steward reminds all passengers to set their watches one hour ahead.

In the morning, the train has reached the *Nullarbor Plain,* passing through the almost barren landscape flickering in the heat outside. Railway buffs are eagerly looking forward to the unique stretch lying ahead, when the Indian-Pacific will travel down the longest absolutely straight piece of track: no less than 478 km without the slightest bend – an ideal occasion for a lengthy exploration of the train.

The less expensive holiday class also has its own saloon and restaurant cars, except that the meals are not included in the price of the ticket. The compartments are somewhat less luxurious and a little smaller, without private toilets. The cars for coach class passengers are equipped with pullman seats and include a special buffet car. Regardless of class, all cars have shower rooms at both ends for the convenience of passengers.

The Indian-Pacific makes its only stop for fuel and water in a small desert town – one of the few settlements along the endless route which are populated by just a handful of railway employees.

It isn't long before the doors are closed again and the Indian-Pacific resumes speed. At some point in the afternoon, there is an announcement over the loudspeakers – an opportunity to register for a sightseeing tour of Adelaide. The capital of South Australia will be reached at 6.30 am the following morning. Later that evening, the bar steward is asked if the excursion will actually be worthwhile. He nods emphatically but adds that he might be partial, being from Adelaide himself. And yes, the train would certainly wait for all those taking part in the tour.

When the train pulls into *Adelaide (p. 87)* station early next morning, a crew of busy helpers immediately begins to clean all the windows, welcomed especially by those passengers who have been trying to take pictures of the landscape from the moving train. The train departs late, and

therefore breakfast is late as well. The jams are getting more and more exotic, however – today, it's rhubarb with champagne. By now, everyone is used to sitting shoulder to shoulder in the crowded dining car.

The train passes through endless wheat fields which soon give way to green hills – seemingly unlimited pasture ground which makes it easy to believe that there are more than 200 million sheep grazing in Australia. But after a while, the green ends, and the train has returned to the Outback once again. Only the big kangaroos and an occasional emu are seen in the steppe. Under a cloudless sky, the Indian-Pacific rolls into the mining town of *Broken Hill.*

That evening, watches are advanced one hour for the last time. Sydney is just a night away. When the sun comes up, the transcontinental silver serpent has reached the Blue Mountains, the favourite summer resort of Sydney folk. In the stations, commuters are waiting for their trains. From higher up in the mountains one can see the skyscrapers of Sydney and even the Pacific in the distance.

Almost on schedule, the train pulls to a stop in the capital of New South Wales, the largest city in Australia and the economic heart of the country. A few minutes later, the big suitcase, which has travelled in the baggage car, is placed on the platform. The journey – one of the last great adventures by train – has come to an end. On the way to the hotel, the taxi driver points to the huge suitcase and the smaller piece of hand luggage and asks: "Coming from Melbourne?" – "From Perth." – "Incredible!" comes his reply. "All the way across the continent. Wouldn't it have been easier to take a plane?"

② TAKING THE ROAD FROM SOUTH TO NORTH

The Stuart Highway is the only asphalted road running through the interior of the Australian continent in a north-south direction. It begins in Port Augusta and ends after some 2,708 km in Darwin. The Stuart Highway passes through all the different climates and landscapes of Australia and is lined with petrol stations and roadhouses – one of the reasons why European visitors in particular like to take this route across the country via Coober Pedy, Alice Springs and Katherine. Plan at least a week for the journey – not counting excursions to Kings Canyon, Ayers Rock, the MacDonnell Ranges and Kakadu National Park.

Planning to cross the entire continent on this their first excursion into the Outback, the Australian couple inquired if kangaroos presented a danger. Most certainly, replied the young lady in the Wadlata Outback Centre at Port Augusta, particularly at dawn and dusk. And do they actually attack people? Of course not, came the reply, the *roos* are actually quite harmless and strict vegetarians. In the early morning and at sundown, however, they tend to be dangerous because they have a tendency to jump in front of approaching vehicles. Many a novice to the Outback was known to have landed in the ditch after colliding with a kangaroo. The Aussies decided to play

it safe and travel only during the daytime. Which is a good idea.

Leaving Port Augusta, you come to a fork in the road. The road going east takes you to the Outback of New South Wales, the road west takes you through the deserted *Nullarbor Plain* to *Perth*. The majority of tourists simply head north, however. From this point onward, the route is called *Stuart Highway* – a pretty big name for a simple two-lane road.

Explorer Highway is what South Australia and the Northern Territory call this route in their joint advertisements directed at holidaymakers. The tourist trade is playing an increasingly bigger role along this former supply route for Aboriginal settlements and Outback farms *(stations)*. *Port Augusta (p. 95)* may have been one of the last cities to benefit, but it is making the most of it now. The local *Wadlata Centre* provides excellent information on the history of the interior and everyday-life in the Outback. And the *Arid Lands Botanical Garden (p. 95)* at the beginning of the Highway is the perfect introduction to the surprisingly rich flora of this desert-like region.

The flood of tourist dollars also brings change to the *road houses* along the highway which all natives between Port Augusta and Darwin simply call *the track.* Where once the drivers of the many-wheeled *road trains* set the tone, you can now hear French, Japanese, Italian and German conversation. But still to be found are the typical old inns and landlords and the traditional long counters with people talking no less than they are drinking.

Pimba is one such stop. The landlord is called Chip by his friends, probably because his predecessor was called Spud. There is no teasing in this nickname but a lot of respect, because Chip has managed to bring rock tours, circus programmes and even a world-music festival to this remote area. For events like this, people come from all over – from neighbouring *Woomera,* a former top-secret missile testing station, from the opal mining town of *Andamooka* and even from *Coober Pedy (p. 117)* further north, another opal town which has become a tourist attraction itself.

The road house in *Marla* is part of a newer generation, designed not so much for cattle farmers but rather for international travellers. The same applies to *Erldunda,* a similarly luxurious stop at the place where almost every tourist vehicle stops – from here, it is just 244 km of good asphalted road to *Ayers Rock (p. 116)* and a little less to *Kings Canyon (p. 115).* Those wishing to travel on the unsurfaced road from the gorge to Alice Springs should take the *Mereenie Loop* through the wilderness in the territory of the Aborigines. Unfortunately, many car rental companies forbid such excursions on these roads. In such a case, there is only one alternative: back to the track and off to *Alice Springs (p. 111).*

You should set aside at least two or three days for this metropolis of the Outback which could easily keep you busy for a week. When you travel on, heading north, make sure to stop at the Ti-Tree and the Barrow Creek road house for a cool drink. At the *Ti-Tree* you should ask about the coffin behind the counter, and at the *Barrow Creek,* cluttered with bric-a-brac, they will gladly tell you how Santa Claus ended up on the roof. The *Wycliffe Well,* not far from the *Devil's Marbles (p. 121),* is worth visiting not only for its 100 different brands of beer and a stuffed gorilla in a four-poster: An artificial lake and a tourist village are scheduled to be created here.

Tennant Creek (p. 120) brings a touch of urbanity to the arid steppe. Along the way, climatic conditions begin to change, and the increasing humidity makes the countryside turn green – it is not far from here to the tropical north with its rainforests. Just beyond the turn-off to the coast via the *Carpentaria Highway* you might want to make a detour to visit the famous *Daly Waters Inn.* This wonderfully cluttered pub is kept alive mostly by tourists, but a lively evening is guaranteed – provided you stick to the drinks. The food is rather forbidding, and the lodgings give a taste of what the Outback must have been like in the 1940s. Similar *good old pubs* are found in *Larrimah* and Mataranka, and the hot springs of *Mataranka (p. 120)* are a good place to cure a hangover.

Katherine (p. 119) is a full-blown city, even if you might see crocodiles crawling along mainstreet during a flood. The pubs are hardly to be recommended, as there are frequent brawls among intoxicated Aborigines. When you come to *Pine Creek,* it is time to make a decision: You can either turn right to *Kakadu National Park (p. 67)* or continue straight ahead to *Darwin (p. 63)* where the Stuart Highway ends.

Practical information

*Useful addresses and information
for your visit to Australia*

ABORIGINES

If you want to visit the Aboriginal reserves, most of which are found in the Northern Territory, you are strictly required to obtain a special pass. For information and applications contact the following addresses: *Northern Land Council, 9 Rowling St., Casuarina, NT 0812, Tel: 08/89 20 51 00;* or *The Central Lands Council, 33 Stuart Hwy., Alice Springs, NT 0871, Tel: 08/89 51 63 20.*

Outback tours led by Aboriginal guides are becoming increasingly popular, particularly with tourists from Europe. You have a choice of anything from short excursions to tours lasting several days. These tours are frequently devoted to special themes, such as "Bush Tucker Trips" where you can learn about wild plants used by the Aborigines for food and medicine. In some places the Aboriginal communities have started to form tourist companies of their own.

ACCOMMODATION

When you are looking for accommodation, you may find that the term hotel is often loosely ap-

plied. In rural areas in particular, the hotel may turn out to be just the local pub, with one or two rooms for guests, but hardly anyone would think of spending the night there. On the other hand, there are pubs which offer very pleasant accommodation. These rooms can be booked in advanced through an agency called *Australian Pubstays.* Away from the cities, most accommodation is in so-called motels.

There are more than 150 youth hostels all over the country. For information contact the *Youth Hostel Association of Australia (YHA, 60 Mary St., Surrey Hills, NSW 2010, Tel: 02/92 12 12 66).*

No membership is required for the private backpacker hostels. They are listed in several different guides, such as the *Backpackers Resort of Australia, 3 Newman St., Nambucca Heads, NSW 2448, Tel: 02/65 68 80 78.*

Bed & breakfast is offered in all parts of the country. There are several organizations which provide comprehensive listings, such as *Bed & Breakfast Australia, 5 Yarabah Av., Gordon, NSW 2072, Tel: 02/94 98 53 44.*

Holiday apartments (self-catering) were first offered in major resort areas only, but now they are found in all larger cities. For a list of addresses contact the local or state-run tourist offices.

Becoming increasingly popular are *farmhouse* holidays, especially on sheep stations or an Outback cattle station. There are several agencies which offer information and reservations, such as *Australian Farmhost and Farm Holidays (P.O. Box 65, Culcairn, NSW 2660, Tel: 02/ 60 29 86 21)* or *Country Life Australia (Taggerty, Vic 3714, Tel: 03/ 57 74 73 02).*

AMERICAN & BRITISH ENGLISH

Marco Polo travel guides are written in British English. In North America, certain terms and usages deviate from British usage. Some of the more frequently encountered examples are:

baggage for luggage, billion for thousand million, cab for taxi, car rental for car hire, drugstore for chemist's, fall for autumn, first floor for groundfloor, freeway/highway for motorway, gas(oline) for petrol, railroad for railway, restroom for toilet/lavatory, streetcar for tram, subway for underground/tube, toll-free numbers for freephone numbers, trailer for caravan, trunk for boot, vacation for holiday, wait staff for waiting staff (in restaurants etc.), zip code for postal code.

ARRIVAL

On arrival in Australia all aircraft are sprayed inside and out with an insecticide which is said to be safe for humans. No passengers are allowed to disembark before this treatment. There are efforts to develop a spray which will stay effective for several years. Other proposals call for the installation of an automatic spraying system in the aircraft.

BANKS & MONEY .

Branches of all main clearing banks, at least in the cities, will change nearly all foreign currencies and also cash travellers cheques but do not usually accept Eurocheques. Banks are also found at all the international airports. Normal banking hours are *Mon–Fri from 9.30 am to 4 pm,* although some branches in the city centres stay open longer. Most international hotels will also change foreign currency, although at less favourable rates. Credit cards are widely used in Australia. Travellers cheques in Australian dollars can be ordered from your local bank before departure.

BUSES

Apart from the usual regional bus companies there are several big companies operating a regularly scheduled, nation-wide overland service, such as *Greyhound Pioneer Australia* or *McCafferty's Express Coaches.* Bus travel is an inexpensive alternative to rail or air travel, especially when taking advantage of the special passes which are offered by these companies for periods of several weeks or even month. As well as their regular scheduled services, the major operators also offer sightseeing tours to a wide range of destinations.

CAMPING

Good, well-furnished campsites exist near all the main tourist destinations, on the outskirts of major cities and in the national

Fire warning – a common sight along country roads in Australia

parks in Australia. Traditional accommodation in tents is usually provided on organized safaris into the Outback with all-terrain vehicles. Apart from that, campers (2–3 beds) or motorhomes (4–8 beds) are becoming increasingly popular. Most campsites are equipped for such vehicles. You can rent fully-equipped campers and motorhomes – not exactly a cheap way to spend your holiday but a very pleasant one. Advance reservations are recommended.

CUSTOMS

Personal items, including cameras, films, etc. may be taken into Australia without payment of duty. Visitors over 18 may also take in duty free 1 litre of alcohol, 250 cigarettes or 250 grams of tobacco plus gifts up to a value of A$ 400. Penalties are severe for anyone taking in drugs and baggage is frequently checked.

There are very strict quarantine laws and the taking in of foodstuffs, fruit, vegetables, seeds and animal and plant products ist prohibited.

DEPARTURE TAX

Upon leaving Australia, every passenger aged 12 years and older is subject to a departure tax of 27 A$ which is usually included in the price of your airline ticket.

DISABLED PERSONS

Modern hotels and residential-complexes are usually equipped for disabled persons, but despite the Australians' general willingness to help, visitors with a disability still face many problems. For information on holiday destinations which are specially equipped for disabled travellers contact the *Australia Council for Rehabilitation for the Disabled (Acrod), P.O. Box 60, Curtin, ACT 2605, Tel: 02/62 82 43 33*

DRIVING

As in the UK, Australians drive on the left-hand side of the road, and all rented cars are right-hand drive. The highway code is similar to that in most European countries. In the Outback you should always be on the lookout for kangaroos, especially at dawn and dusk – they have a nasty habit of suddenly jumping in front of approaching cars.

Visitors may drive in Australia with a valid licence from their home country. In order to rent a car you need to be at least 21, in some cases 25 years of age. If you do not have a major credit card or a *Rental Car Voucher* from a tour operator, you will be required to pay for the car in advance.

Collision damage insurance is usually included in your rental contract. If you plan return the car to a different station, you will be charged extra in most cases. Fuel is sold by the litre and is relatively cheap in Australia. In rural areas and in the suburban areas of the larger cities, petrol stations often close as early as 5 pm.

EMBASSIES/CONSULATES

British High Commission
Commonwealth Av., Yarralumla, Canberra; Tel: 06/270 66 66; Mon–Fri 9–12 am and 2–4 pm

British Consulate General
Gateway Plaza, 1 Macquarie Place, Sydney; Tel: 02/247 75 21; Mon–Fri 10 am–3 pm

U.S. Embassy
21 Moonah Place, Yarralumla, Canberra; Tel: 06/270 50 00; Mon–Fri 8.30–12.30 am

U.S. Consulate General
19–29 Martin Place, Sydney: Tel: 02/373 92 00; Mon–Fri 8.30–11 am

Canadian High Commission
Commonwealth Av., Yarralumla, Canberra; Tel: 06/273 38 44

EMERGENCY

Australia has set up a nation-wide system of emergency services which can be called free of charge from any telephone by dialling 000. The operator will connect you with the police, the fire department or the paramedics.

FLIGHTS

Australia has very good domestic air service which was deregulated in 1991. *Qantas* and *Ansett,* the two major domestic carriers, are now involved in a price war which is intensified by a number of new budget airlines. All domestic flights are strictly non-smoking flights. *Ansett, Quantas* and *East-West* offer reduced air passes to foreign visitors.

If you plan to fly to the Outback you are required to charter light aircarft as there is no scheduled service. Every settlement and nearly every station (farm) has its own runway. The cost of chartering a plane is significantly lower than in Europe.

IMMIGRATION

Australia is still a popular destination for immigration, although the government has now adopted a much more restrictive policy than before. For further information contact the Australian Embassy.

INFORMATION

Australian Tourist Commission
www.aussie.net.au
In the UK:
Gemini House, 10–18 Poutney Hill, London, SW 15 6AA; Tel: 0181/780 22 29, Fax: 0181/780 14 96

In the U.S.A.:
New York, 25th floor, 100 Park Av. New York, NY 10017; Tel: (212) 687-6300, Fax: (212) 661 33 40
In Canada:
Contact the New York office
New South Wales Tourism Office
www.tourism.nsw.gov.au
(see Australian Tourism Commission)
Queensland Tourist & Travel Corporation
Queensland House, 392/3 London. WC2R OLZ; Tel: 0171/240 05 25, Fax: 0171/836 58 81
www.queensland-holidays.com.au
Tourism Victoria
Victoria House, Melbourne Place, The Strand, London, WC2B 4LG; Tel: 0171/240 71 76, Fax: 0171/ 240 71 96
www.tourism.vic.gov.au
Northern Territory
Same address as South Australia Tourism; Tel: 0181/944 29 92, Fax: 0181/944 29 93
www.nttc.com.au
South Australia Tourism
1st floor, Beaumont House, Lambton Rd., London, SW20 OLW; Melbourne Place, The Strand London, WC2B 4LG; Tel: 0181/944 53 75, Fax: 0181/944 53 76
www.tourism.sa.gov.au
Tasmania
www.tourism.tas.gov.au
Western Australia Tourism
Western Australia House, 115 The Strand, London, WC2R OAJ; Tel: 0171/240 28 81, Fax: 0173/379 98 26
www.wa.gov.au/gov/watc

MEDICAL SERVICE

Most urban regions in Australia are well supplied with doctors. British travellers are generally covered by their Medicare scheme, but this is only intended to provide emergency aid. All visitors are recommended to take out extra medical and accident insurance. In the Outback you can always rely on the Royal Flying Doctor Service which can be contacted by radio any time. In all cities it is safe to drink tap water. Australian pharmacies are called *Chemists.* Inoculations are not required unless you come from a third world country which is considered a high-risk area for certain types of diseases.

NEWSPAPERS

The most renowned daily papers are published in the two largest cities – the "Sydney Morning Herald" and the "Melbourne Age". Another respected national daily is the "Australian". In most local papers you will find helpful information on events of all kinds – usually in the Thursday and Friday editions. There are also weeklies in a number of other European languages, as one would expect in a country with so many immigrants.

OPENING TIMES

Most offices are open *Mon–Fri 9 am–5 pm, most shops stay open to 5.30 pm on weekdays and to midday on Saturdays.* Most cities have one day for late-night shopping when stores stay open to 9 pm. More and more shops are also beginning to open on Sundays.

OUTBACK

Tours into the Australian Outback call for careful preparation. One of the essential requirements is a plentiful supply of drinking water. When exploring the national parks away from the main routes, it is advisable to register with the rangers before you set out. If you plan to head for the Outback off the beaten track you should also make sure that somebody knows where you are going. When heading out overland, four-wheel drive vehicles are indispensable. In the tropical north, many tracks during rainy season, and even asphalt roads often stay flooded for days. In case of a breakdown it is advised that you stay with your car instead of heading out on foot by yourself. You will be spotted more easily from the air if you are near the car, and will also save energy and at least have some shade. When hiking, be sure to wear strong boots which will also protect you against snakes. Some sort of headgear is also essential to protect you from the sun.

PASSPORT/VISA

All visitors to Australia require a passport, and all except New Zealanders must also have a visa which is free for a stay of up to three months. If you intend to stay for a longer time, you will be charged for a long-term visa. When travelling on a tourist visa you are not allowed to work in Australia. Backpackers who intend to take on odd jobs in order to enhance their budget need a special visa which is usually valid for six months. Application forms can be obtained at any embassy or consulate. Processing generally takes only a few days, but if you are in hurry, you can go directly to an embassy or consulate near you where you will get a visa usually within

hours (be sure to go in the morning). Adresses:

Australian High Commision
Australia House, The Strand, London, WC2B 4LA; Tel: 0171/379 43 34, Fax: 0171/465 82 10

Australian Consulate
Chatsworth House, Lever St, Manchester, M12Dl; Tel: 0161/228 13 44, Fax: 0161/236 40 74

United States:
Australian Embassy
Washington DC, Tel: 797-3000, Fax: 797-3168

Australian Consulate
New York, NY; Tel: 408-8400, Fax: 408-8401

Australian Embassy
Loss Angeles, CA; Tel: 469-4300, Fax: 622-6924

Canada:
The Australian Embassy
Suite 710, 50 O'Connor Street, Ottawa; Tel: 236 08 41

PHOTOGRAPHY

Films and video films are usually more expensive in Australia than in most European countries. Colour prints can be developed within 24 hours, and sometimes within one hour, in most cities. All major manufactures have set up processing centres for slides as well – addresses are provided by any photography shop.

POST/TELEPHONES

The postal service and the communication services are separate companies in Australia, so you

These makeshift toilets are becoming increasingly rare in the Outback

cannot go to the post office to make a long-distance phone call, but you can make international calls from any public telephone. The only exception are the red phones which are exclusively for local calls and accept only 10 or 20 cent coins. To make an international call, you must dial 00 11 followed by the country code – 44 for the UK, 1 for the U.S. and Canada and 353 for Ireland – plus the area code (omitting the 0) and the subscriber phone number you want to call. When making an international call to Australia, the applicable country code is 61, again followed by the area code (omitting the 0) and the local number.

An important reminder: Australia is currently in the process of changing all telephone number to at least 8 digits. The area code numbers are also being changed – each state will be given a separate area code. Most changes have already been included in this guide.

Post offices are usually open *Mon–Fri 9 am–5 pm.* They also sell envelopes and packaging materials. Stamp collectors will find special post offices in the big cities.

RESTAURANTS AND PUBS

Restaurants which do not have a licence to sell alcoholic beverages are classified as BYO *(bring your own)* – which means you are welcome to bring beer or wine as you please. As alcohol licences are expensive, most BYO restaurants tend to be less expensive. Alcoholic beverages can be bought in a *liquor store* or in a *bottle shop* at some hotels. Most restaurants serve alcoholic beverages *only between 10 am and midnight (10 pm on Sun),* but licensing regulations vary from one state to the next. Remember that when someone buys you a drink, it is customary that you buy the next round.

TAXIS

In the major cities taxis are required to have meters, but in rural areas the fare is agreed in advance. As a rule, taxi drivers charge reasonable prices. You can recognize taxis which are available for rent by their illuminated roof light. Expect to pay a small extra charge for luggage.

TIME ZONES

The Australian continent is divided into three time zones. The first is *Eastern Standard Time (EST = CET + 9 hours)* on the east coast in the states of Queensland, New South Wales, Victoria and Tasmania. The second is *Central Standard Time (CST) which* is 30 minutes behind EST and is observed in South Australia and the Northern Territory. And finally, *Western Standard Time (WST)* which is two hours behind EST and is observed in Western Australia. In the Australian summer, most states go over to summer time, setting the clock one hour ahead. Except in summer time, the east coast of Australia is nine hours ahead of Europe.

TIPPING

Tipping is not a wide-spread practice in Australia. Hotel staff, hairdressers and taxi drivers do not expect a tip, although taxi passengers usually round up the fare to the nearest full dollar. In the better restaurants, a tip of about 10 per cent of the amount is considered adequate.

TRAINS

Australia does not have a dense network of railways, but there are a number of excellent long-distance trains. Most of the bigger cities have a good suburban and regional rail service. Foreign visitors have a choice of two very economical rail passes, the *Austrailpass* for unlimited travel on the entire rail network within a certain period of time, and the *Austrail-Flexipass* which can be used on a given number of days within a certain period, e.g. 30 days of travel within six months. Prices vary according to the period of validity. *For information contact Railways of Australia, 85 Queen St., Melbourne, Vic 3000, Tel: 03/96 08 08 11, or Rail Australia in the UK, Tel: 01733/33 55 99*

VOLTAGE

Electricity is supplied at 240/250 Volts AC. Note that the plugs used in Australia have different prongs, so you will need a special adapter if you plan to use your own appliances. These adapters can be bought in most cities but are usually not available in rural areas.

WEIGHTS & MEASURES

1 cm	0.39 inch
1 m	1.09 yd (3.28 ft)
1 km	0.62 miles
1 sq m	1.20 sq yds
1 ha	2.47 acres
1 sq km	0.39 sq miles
1 g	0.035 ounces
1 kg	2.21 pounds
1 British tonne	1.016 kg
1 US ton	907 kg

1 litre is equivalent to 0.22 Imperial gallons and 0.26 US gallons.

WHEN TO GO

As the seasons in the southern hemisphere are opposite to those in the northern half of the globe,

Australians celebrate Christmas in the summer, and January is the warmest month. During the Australian summer, many of the hotels, planes and trains are usually fully booked, and prices tend to be higher than during the rest of the year. In terms of both climate and prices, November and February/March are ideal months for travelling. In winter, i.e. in July and August, the Australian south coast can be particularly wet and cold and generally unpleasant.

Frost is rare, however. In the subtropical regions and in the tropical north, seasonal differences are less pronounced. Note, however, that there is a rainy season from November to March. During off-peak seasons, the airlines usually offer substantially reduced fares. In view of the ozone layer depletion and the intensity of solar radiation you should not expose your skin to the sun too long and make sure you use sun protection with a high sun-block factor.

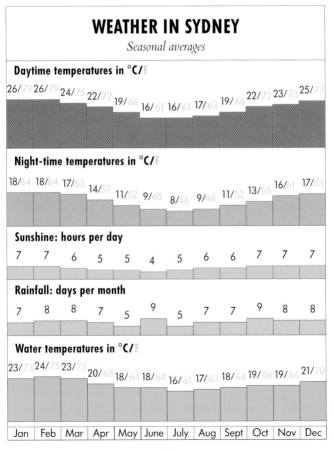

WEATHER IN SYDNEY
Seasonal averages

Daytime temperatures in °C/F

Jan	Feb	Mar	Apr	May	June	July	Aug	Sept	Oct	Nov	Dec
26/79	26/79	24/75	22/72	19/66	16/61	16/61	17/63	19/66	22/72	23/73	25/77

Night-time temperatures in °C/F

| 18/64 | 18/64 | 17/63 | 14/57 | 11/52 | 9/48 | 8/46 | 9/48 | 11/52 | 13/55 | 16/61 | 17/63 |

Sunshine: hours per day

| 7 | 7 | 6 | 5 | 5 | 4 | 5 | 6 | 6 | 7 | 7 | 7 |

Rainfall: days per month

| 7 | 8 | 8 | 7 | 5 | 9 | 5 | 7 | 7 | 9 | 8 | 8 |

Water temperatures in °C/F

| 23/73 | 24/75 | 23/73 | 20/68 | 18/64 | 18/64 | 16/61 | 17/63 | 18/64 | 19/66 | 19/66 | 21/70 |

| Jan | Feb | Mar | Apr | May | June | July | Aug | Sept | Oct | Nov | Dec |

Do's and don'ts

*Some hints about possible dangers
and things you should avoid*

Aborigines

Australians are quite aware of the fact that their ancestors did not have much respect for the Aborigines. And they also know that in today's society, Aborigines do not have the same opportunities as the white Australians. But there is a widespread view that the government is doing quite enough by providing all sorts of costly aid, and so they do not appreciate foreigners reproaching them for the way the Aborigines are treated. Likewise, the Aborigines themselves also do not appreciate tourists bringing up the matter.

Convicts

Some visitors think it funny to speak of Australians as "descendants of convicts." Aussies certainly have a sense of humour but it is easy to understand that they do not take kindly to this kind of mockery. Having been looked down upon by the British for their backwoods mentality for so long in the past they are somewhat sensitive when foreigners poke fun at their ancestry.

Opals

Australia is one of the world's leading producers of diamonds but it is probably even more famous for its opals. These semiprecious stones are mainly found at *Coober Pedy* and *Andamooka (SA)* and in *Lightning Ridge (NSW)*. In practically all the tourist centres you will find opal dealers looking for customers. Many of them are legitimate dealers, but some are trying to sell lowgrade stones. So when faced with more expensive gems you should consult an independent expert before buying. Most opals are light coloured or milky with shiny inclusions. Black opals are only found at Lightning Ridge. All dealers also offer less expensive triplets in which only one of the layers is actually opal.

Politics

It has long been part of the Australian lifestyle to invite friends in to one's house, especially for a barbecue in the garden, and this hospitality is shared with many visitors also. In such a situation, guests should refrain from talking politics for too long. Politics is certainly not a subject matter that is considered taboo, but Australians are not all that concerned with what their politicians do. In most cases you may hear them condemning high taxes and calling politicians names, but they usually let it go at that.

ROAD ATLAS LEGEND

▬▬▬	Autobahn mit Anschlußstelle Motorway with junction
Datum, Date Date, Data	Autobahn in Bau Motorway under construction
▬▬▬	Autobahn in Planung Motorway projected
▬▬▬	Durchgangsstraße Thoroughfare
▬▬▬	Durchgangsstraße unbefestigt (Auswahl) Thoroughfare unsealed (selection)
▬▬▬	Hauptstraße Main road
▬▬▬	Hauptstraße unbefestigt (Auswahl) Main road unsealed (selection)
▬▬▬	Sonstige Straße, Piste Other road, track
▬▬▬	Pisten Tracks
→ ←	Straßentunnel Road tunnel
▬ ▬	Straßen in Bau Roads under construction
31 A2	Straßennummern Road numbers
480	Fernkilometer Very long distances in km
49	Großkilometer Long distances in km
10	Kleinkilometer Short distances in km
▬▬▬	Fernverkehrsbahn Main line railway
▬ ▬ ▬	Sonstige Eisenbahn Secondary line railway
▬▬●	Autofähre Car ferry
▬ ▬ ▬	Schiffahrtslinie Shipping route
592	Paß mit Höhenangabe Pass with height
< <	Bedeutende Steigungen Important gradients
2228 ▲	Bergspitze mit Höhenangabe in Metern Mountain top with height in metres
CANBERRA	Hauptstadt Capital
PERTH	Verwaltungssitz Administrative capital
▭▭▭	Staatsgrenze National boundary
▭▭▭	Verwaltungsgrenze Administrative boundary

Kultur
Culture

★★ <u>CAIRNS</u>	
★★ <u>Ubirr Rock</u>	Eine Reise wert Worth a journey
★ <u>BALLARAT</u>	
★ <u>Old Sydney Town</u>	Lohnt einen Umweg Worth a detour

Landschaft
Landscape

★★ **Blue Mtns.**	
★★ <u>Ayers Rock</u>	Eine Reise wert Worth a journey
★ **Flinders Range**	
★ <u>Ormiston Gorge</u>	Lohnt einen Umweg Worth a detour

▭	Nationalpark, Naturpark, Naturschutzgebiet National park, nature park, nature reserve
▭	Aboriginal-Schutzgebiet Aboriginal reserve
▭	Sperrgebiet Prohibited area
～～	Fluß, ganzjährig River, permanent
⌐¬	Fluß, periodisch River, periodic
◯	Süßwassersee Freshwater lake
◌	Salzsee Saltwater lake
≈≈	Sumpf Swamp
≈≈	Salzsumpf Saltwater swamp
⬚	Korallenriff Coral reef
	Wüste Desert
·	Farm, Station Homestead, station
♪	Schloß, Burg Palace, castle
⊥	Denkmal Monument
╱	Wasserfall Waterfall
∩	Höhle Cave
∴	Ruinenstätte Ruins
▪	Sonstiges Objekt Other object
✦	Verkehrsflughafen Airport
⊕	Flugplatz Airfield

Road Atlas of Australia

*Please refer to back cover for an overview
of this Road Atlas*

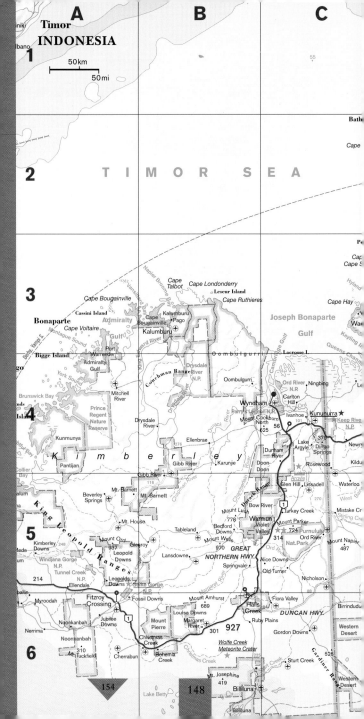

INDONESIA
Timor

TIMOR SEA

1

50km
50mi

2

3

Cape Bougainville
Cassini Island
Bonaparte
Cape Voltaire
Montague Sound
Port Warrender
Admiralty Gulf
Bigge Island
York Sound

Cape Talbot
Cape Londonderry
Leseur Island
Cape Ruthieres
Kalumburu
Pago
Kalumburu
Oombulgurri

Joseph Bonaparte Gulf
Cape Hay
Keeling I.
Queens Channel
Lacrosse I.
Cambridge Gulf

4

Brunswick Bay
Island
Prince Regent Nature Reserve
Kunmunya
Pantijan
Collier Bay

Mitchell River
Drysdale River
Couchman Range
Drysdale River N.P.
Ellenbrae
Gibb River
Karunjie
Doon Doon

Drysdale River N.P.
Oombulgurri
Wyndham
Parry's Lagoon N.R.
Mount Cockburn North 625
Durack River
Dunham River
Glen Hill
Rosewood

Carlton Hill
Ord River N.R.
Ningbing
Ivanhoe
Kununurra
Keep River N.P.
Newry
Lake Argyle
Dingo Springs
Lissadell
Waterloo
West

5

King Leopold Ranges
Kimberley Downs 248
Medi
Windjana Gorge N.P.
Tunnel Creek 214
N.P.
Ellendale
Myroodah
Naonkanbah
Nerrima
Noonkanbah
Mt. Tuckfield 310

Beverley Springs
Mt. Barnett 116
Mt. Barnett
Mt. House
Mount Ord 937
Gleeroy
Leopold Downs
Lansdowne
Tableland
Bedford Downs
Mount Wells
Fitzroy Crossing
Jubilee Downs
Mount Pierre
Christmas Creek

Mount Lush
Warmun
Violet Valley
Springvale
Alice Downs
Old Turner
Leopolds Downs
Geikie Gorge N.P.
Fossil Downs
Mount Amhurst 689
Louisa Downs
Margaret River 301
Halls Creek
Ruby Plains
927
Bohemia Creek
Wolfe Creek Meteorite Crater
Christmas Creek

Bow River
Turkey Creek
Mount Parker 724
Purnululu 314
Ord River Nat.Park
Nicholson
Flora Valley
DUNCAN HWY.
Gordon Downs
Mount Napier 487
Mistake Cr
Stirling Cr

GREAT NORTHERN HWY.
Margaret River

DUNCAN HWY.
Western Desert
Birrindudu
Western Desert
Gardner Ra
626

Mt. Josephine 419
Lake Betty
Billiluna
Billiluna

154   148

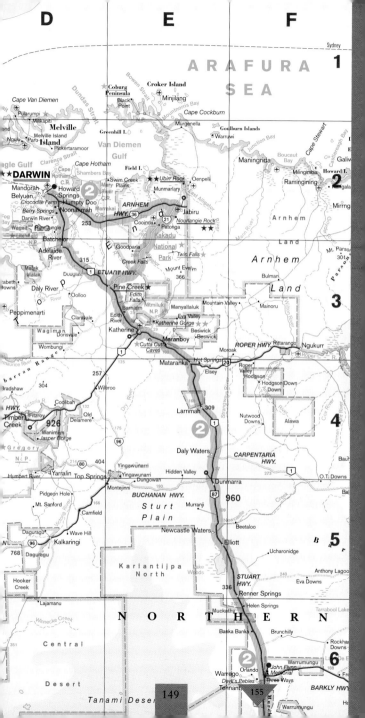

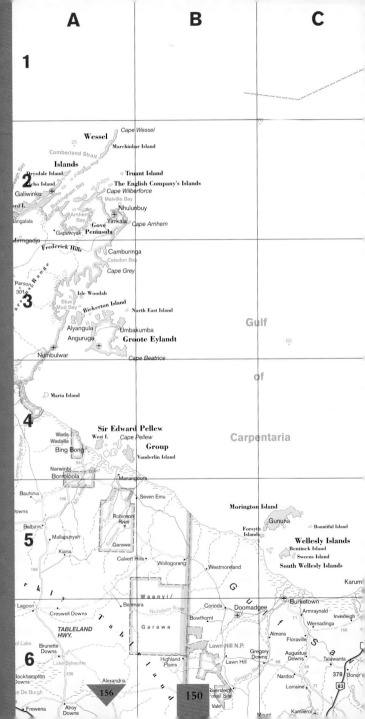

A **B** **C**

1

2

Cape Wessel
Wessel
Marchinbar Island
Cumberland Strait
Islands
Drysdale Island
Echo Island
○ Truant Island
Galiwinku
The English Company's Islands
Cape Wilberforce
Melville Bay
Nhulunbuy
Yirrkala
Cape Arnhem
ard I.
Buckingham Bay
Arnhem Bay
Mirrngadja
Gapuwiyak
Gove Peninsula
Jangalala

3

Frederick Hills
Camburinga
Caledon Bay
Cape Grey
Parsons
301
Range
Isle Woodah
Blue
Mud Bay
Bickerton Island
● North East Island
Alyangula
Anguruga
Umbakumba
Groote Eylandt
Numbulwar
Cape Beatrice

Gulf
65

4

◌ Maria Island
of
Carpentaria
Wada
Wadalla
Sir Edward Pellew
West I. Cape Pellew
Group
Bing Bong
Vanderlin Island
Narwinbi
Borroloola
Manangoora

5

Bauhinia
Downs
106
Peach River
Seven Emu
Morington Island
Gununa
Balbirini
Mallapunyah
Robinson
River
○ Bountiful Island
Robinson
Forsyth
Islands
Wellesly Islands
Kiana
Garawa
Bentinck Island
Sweens Island
Calvert Hills
Wollogorang
Westmoreland
South Wellesly Islands
Karum
156
Waanyi/
Corinda
Lagoon
Benmara
Nicholson River
Doomadgee
Burketown
Creswell Downs
Garawa
Bowthornt
Armraynald
Inverleigh
TABLELAND
Wernadinga
160
HWY.
l
a
n
d
Almora
Brunette
Downs
Lake Sylvester
Floraville
Augustus
Downs
Talawanta
ol Lake
226
Highland
Plains
Lawn Hill N.P.
Gregory
Downs
68
59
378 Donor'
Rockhampton
Downs
Lawn Hill
Nardoo
Lorraine
77
83
De Burgh
Alexandria
156
Riversleigh
Fossil Site
Frewena
Alroy
Downs
150
Vale
Mount
Kamileroi

Buckingham Bay
Parsons
Cape Pellew
McArthur River
Calvert River
Robinson River
Gregory River
71
f
S

25
70
54

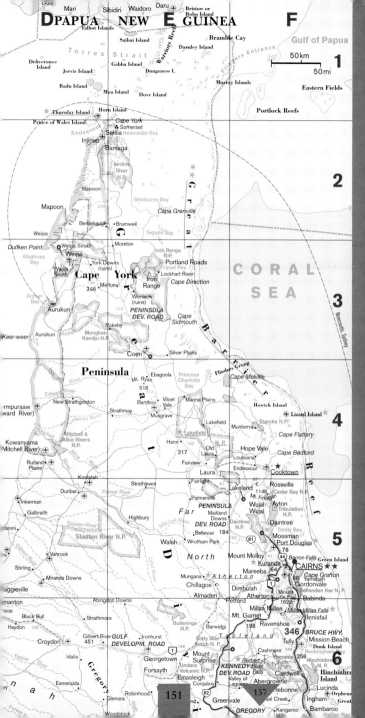

Mari
Sibidiri
Waidoro
Daru
Bristow or
Bobo Island

Talbot Islands
Saibai Island
Bramble Cay
Darnley Island
Gulf of Papua
F

Torres Strait
Barrier Reefs
Flinders Entrance
50km
50mi
1

Deliverance
Island
Jervis Island
Gabba Island
Dungeness I.
Murray Islands
Eastern Fields

Badu Island
Moa Island
Dove Island
Portlock Reefs

Thursday Island
Horn Island
Prince of Wales Island
Cape York
Somerset
Newcastle Bay
Portlock Reefs

Endeavour Strait
Seisia
Injinoo
Bamaga
2

Mapoon
Jardine
River
N.P.
Shelburne Bay
Cape Grenville

Mapoon
Berbiehaugh
Bramwell
Temple Bay

Weipa
Moreton
Iron Range
N.P.

Duifken Point
Weipa South
Weipa
Portland Roads
Lockhart River
C O R A L

Albatross
Bay
York Downs
(ruins)
Iron
Range
Cape Direction
S E A

Weipa
South
Cape York
Merluna
Wenlock
(ruins)
Cape Sidmouth
3

Archer
Bay
Aurukun
246
112
PENINSULA
DEV. ROAD

Keer-weer
Aurukun
Archer
Mungkan
Kandju N.P.
Rokeby
Coen
Silver Plains

Peninsula
Mt. Ryan
518
Ebagoola
Princess
Charlotte
Bay
Flinders Group
Cape Melville

rmpuraaw
ward River)
New Strathgordon
Bamboo
Viloet
Vale
Marina Plains
Howick Island
Lizard Island
4

Strathmay
Musgrave
Lakefield
Munberra
Starcke N.P.
Cape Flattery

Kowanyama
Mitchell River)
Mitchell &
Alice Rivers
N.P.
Hann
143
Old
Laura
N.P.
Hope Vale
Louisiana
Cape Bedford

Rutland
Plains
317
Fairview
Laura
Endeavour
Cooktown

Koolatah
Fairlight
Lakeland
Rossville
Mt. Finlay
1148

Dunbar
Strathleven
Palmer River
Palmerville
PENINSULA
DEV. ROAD
Wujal
Wujal
Ayton
5

Inkerman
Galbraith
Highbury
Maitland
Downs
Bellevue
184
Daintree
N.P.
Daintree
Trinity Bay
Mossman
Port Douglas

caroni
Vanrook
Staaten River N.P.
Walsh
Wrotham Park
Far
North
Mount Molloy
78
Kuranda
44
Barron Falls
Green Island
CAIRNS

Stirling
Miranda Downs
Lynd River
Mungana
Atherton
Mareeba
64
Cape Grafton
Gordonvale
Yarrabah

aggieville
Chillagoe
Dimbulah
Almaden
Petford
Atherton
Mount
1622
Babinda
Bellenden Ker N.P.

anton
ncoe
Black Bull
Abingdon Downs
Strathmore
Bullerinja
N.P.
Barwidgi
Millaa Millaa
Mt. Garnet
198
Ravenshoe
Millaa Millaa Falls
Innisfail
D
346
BRUCE HWY.
Mission Beach

Haydon
155
Croydon
Gilbert River
451
Ironhurst
148
GULF
DEVELOPM. ROAD
Georgetown
Forty Mile
Scrub N.P.
Tableland
Tully
Rockingham
258
Hinchinbrook
Island

Idalia
Mount
Surprise
Forsayth
Einasleigh
Conjuboy
Undara
Volcanic N.P.
KENNEDY
DEV. ROAD
Herbert
River
Falls
Cashmere
Valley of
Lagoons
Cardwell
Abergowrie
Lucinda
Orpheus
Island

Black Bull
Esmeralda
Glenora
Robinhood
Woodstock
Greenvale
151
157
GREGORY
Kangaroo
Ingham
Bambaroo
Halifax

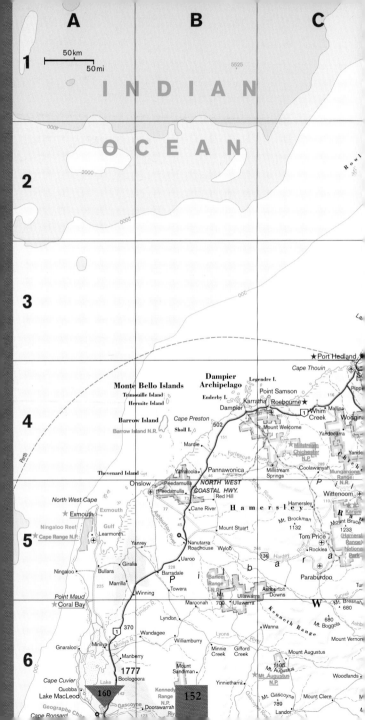

1

50 km
50 mi

I N D I A N

5525

O C E A N

2

Rowl

4000

2000

2000

3

200

La

★ Port Hedland

Cape Thouin

Dampier
Archipelago

Legendre I.

S.

Monte Bello Islands

Trimouille Island
Hermite Island

Enderby I.

Point Samson

Pippe

Karratha ★ Roebourne ★

116

Mallina

4

Barrow Island

Barrow Island N.R.

Cape Preston

Dampier

1

Whim
Creek

Wodgina

502

Sholl I.

Mount Welcome

Yandearra

Yande

Mardie

151

Fortescue River

Millstream
Chichester
N.P.

Chich

Thevenard Island

Yarraloola

Pannawonica

Millstream
Springs

Coolawanyah

289

Mungaroona
Range
N.R.

Perth

Onslow

Peedamulla
Peedamulla

NORTH WEST
COASTAL HWY.

Red Hill

P

Wittenoom

110

5

North West Cape

Exmouth

★ Exmouth

73

Cane River

H a m e r s l e y

Hamersley

Karijini

R

Ningaloo Reef

Cape Range N.P.

Learmonth

Gulf

77

Mt. Brockman

1132

Mt Bruce
1233

(Hamersley
Range)
Nationa
Park

45

Mount Stuart

Yanrey

Nanutarra
Roadhouse

Wyloo

246

Tom Price

Rocklea

a

r

a

136

Hardey

Ningaloo

Bullara

Giralia

Uaroo

228

Paraburdoo

Barradale

P

i

Towera

700

b

a

Tur

Point Maud

Marrilla

Winning

Barlee
Range
N.P.

Mt.

Ashburton
Downs

W

Mt. Bresnah

★ Coral Bay

225

Maroonah

Ullawarra
Ullawarra

Kenneth Range

680
Mt. Boggola

Ashb

Lyndon R.

Lyndon

Lyons

Wanna

Mount Vernon

6

Cape Cuvier

Quobba

1

370

Gnaraloo

Minilya

Minilya R.

Wandagee

Williambury

Minnie
Creek

Gifford
Creek

Mount Augustus

Manberry

1777

Boologoora

Mount
Sandiman

1105
Mt. Augustus
Mt. Augustus
N.P.

Woodlands

Lake MacLeod

160

Geographe Cha

Cape Bonsard

142

Kennedy
Range
N.P.

152

Doorawarrah

Yinnietharra

Gascoyne

Mt. Gascoyne
789

Mount Clere

Landor

173

Lake

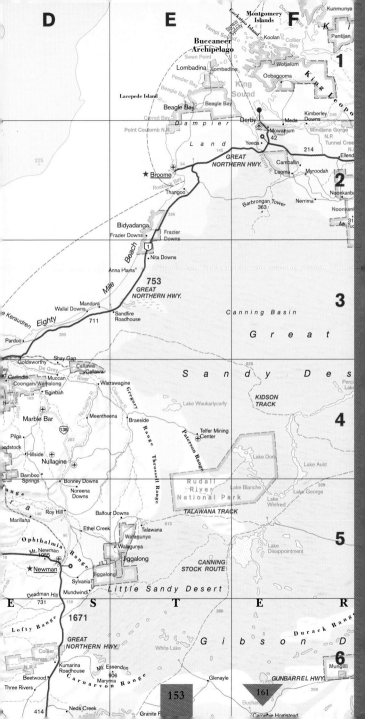

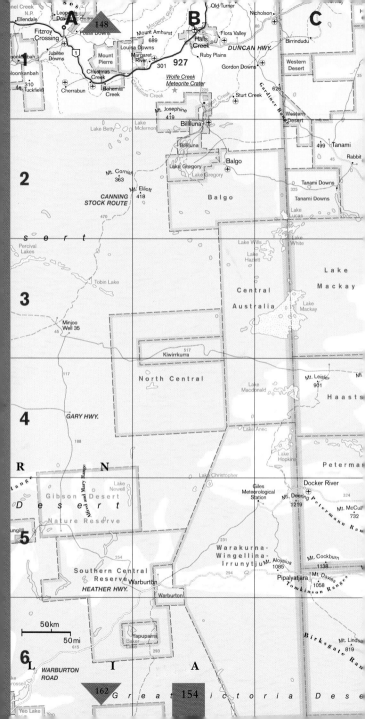

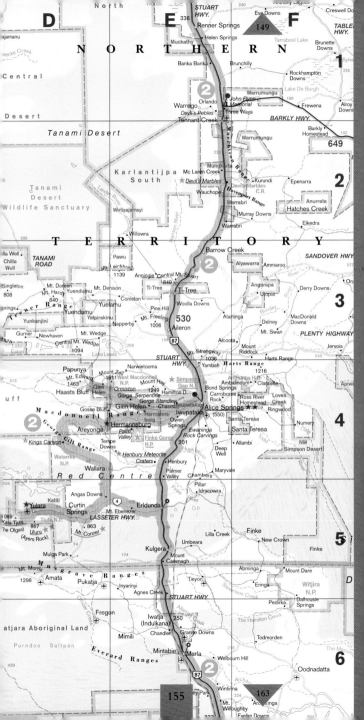

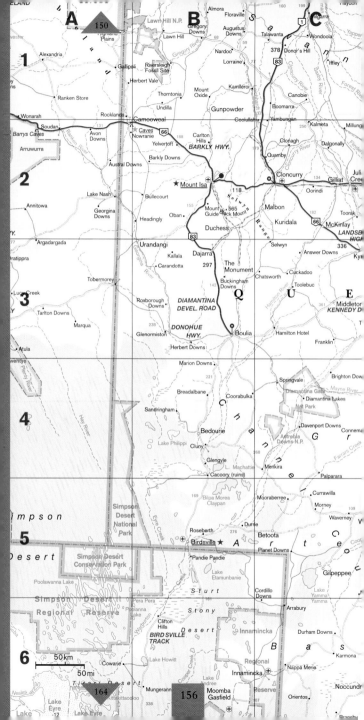

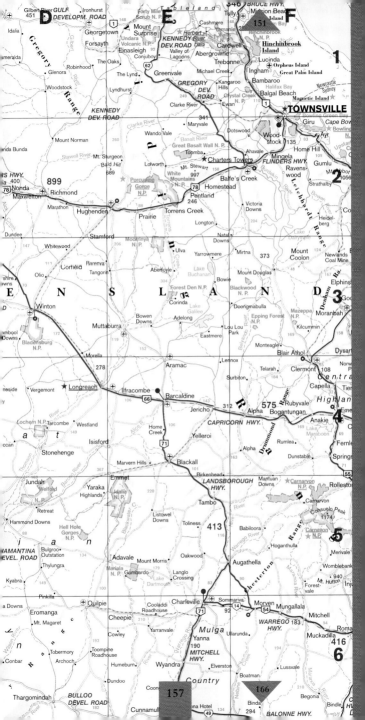

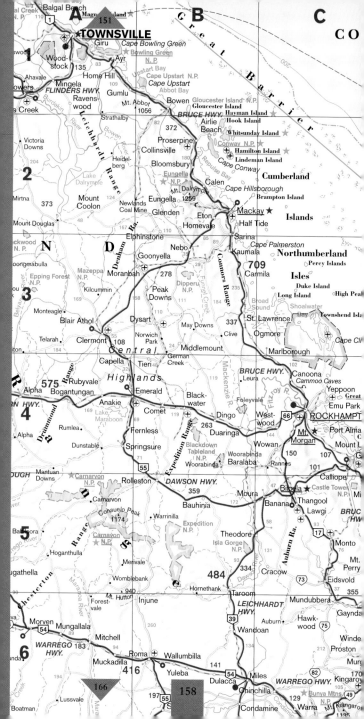

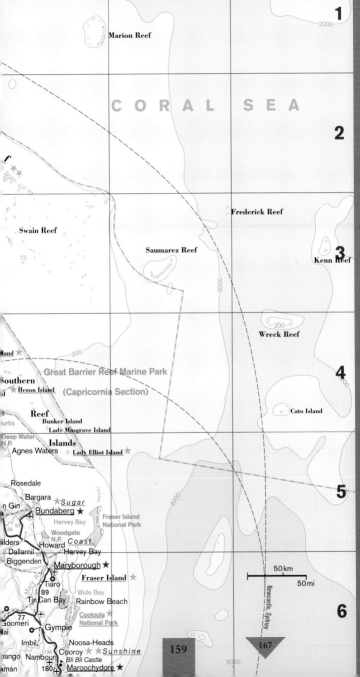

D   **E**   **F**

1

Marion Reef

C O R A L   S E A

2

Frederick Reef

Swain Reef

Saumarez Reef

Kenn Reef

3

Wreck Reef

Great Barrier Reef Marine Park

Southern

Heron Island   (Capricornia Section)

4

Reef

Cato Island

Bunker Island
Lady Musgrave Island

Deep Water
N.P.

Islands

Agnes Waters   Lady Elliot Island

Rosedale

Bargara

n Gin   *Sugar*
Bundaberg ★

Hervey Bay   Fraser Island
National Park

Woodgate
N.P.
Howard   *Coast*

lders
Dallarnil   Hervey Bay
Biggenden

Maryborough ★

Tiaro

89

Tin Can Bay   *Fraser Island* ★

Rainbow Beach   Wide Bay

77   Cooloola
National Park

oomeri   Gympie

Imbil   Noosa-Heads

ango   Nambour   Cooroy ★ ★ *Sunshine*
Bli Bli Castle

man   180   Maroochydore ★

5

Newcastle, Sydney

50km
50mi

6

167

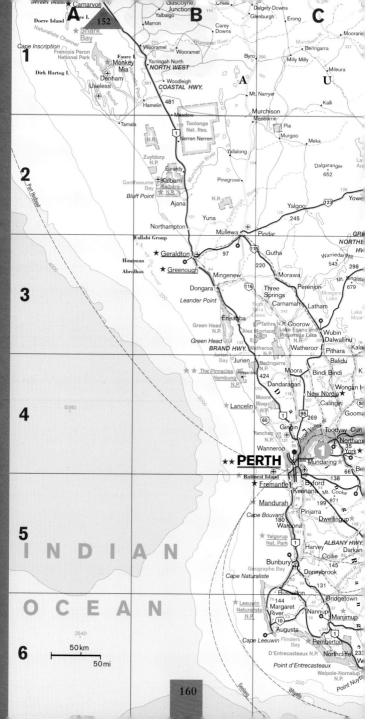

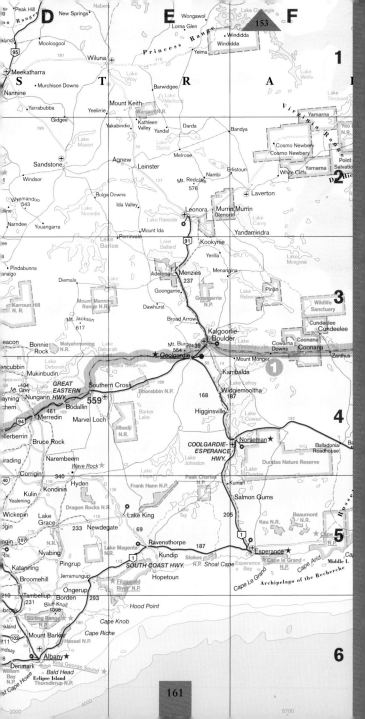

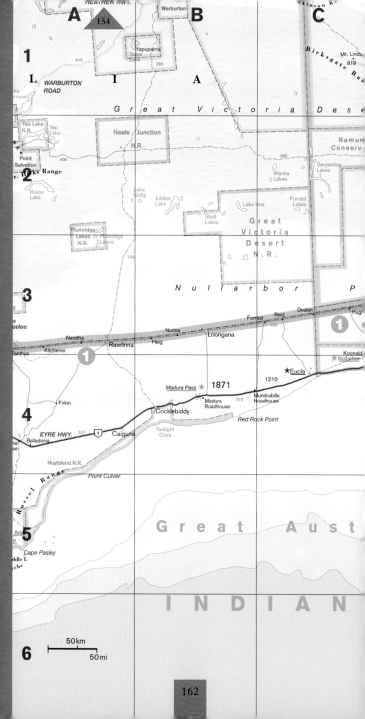

A 154 B C

1

L

WARBURTON ROAD

615

Warburton

I

Yapuparra
Baker
Lake

293

A

Birksgate Ra

Mt. Linds.
819

G r e a t   V i c t o r i a   D e s e

2

Yeo Lake
N.R.

Yeo
Lake

Neale   Junction
N.R.

Point
Salvation

r. Hicks Range

400

Rason
Lake

Lake
Gidgi

Jubilee
Lake

Shell
Lakes

Wanna
Lakes

600

Serpentine
Lakes

Namu
Conserv

Lake Ima

Forrest
Lakes

G r e a t
V i c t o r i a
D e s e r t
N . R .

Plumridge
Lakes N.R.

Plumridge
Lakes

330

3

eelee

N u l l a r b o r

P

Forrest   Reid   Deakin

Hugh

600

1

Naretha

Kitchener

Zanthus

Rawlinna   Haig

Nurina

Loongana

1

Koonald
Nullarbor

4

Firkin

Madura Pass ★   **1871**

Cocklebiddy

Madura
Roadhouse

1210   ★ Eucla

Mundrabilla
Roadhouse

275

EYRE HWY.   247   ①   Caiguna

Balladonia

Twilight
Cove

Red Rock Point

Nuytsland N.R.

Russel Range

Point Culver

5

Aria

ddle I.

che

Cape Pasley

G r e a t   A u s t

6

50km
50mi

I N D I A N

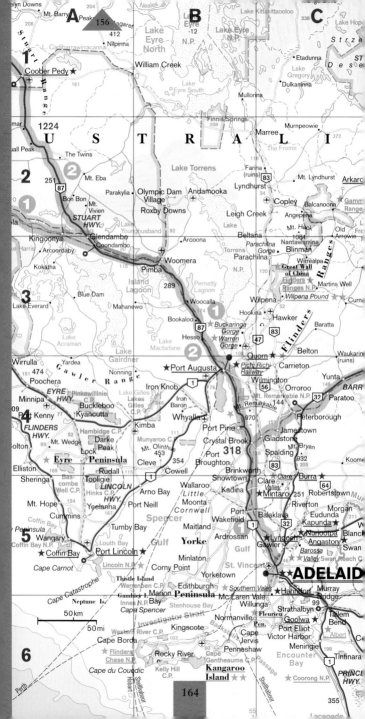

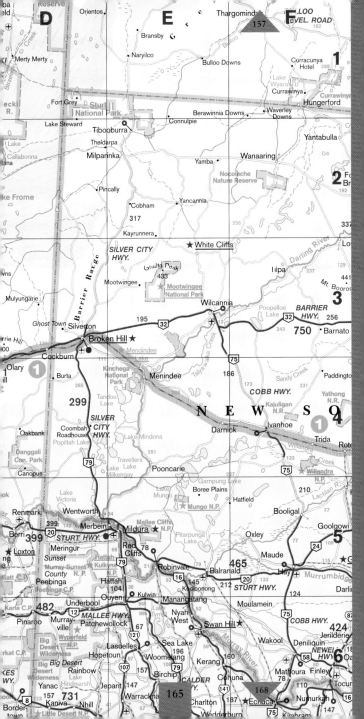

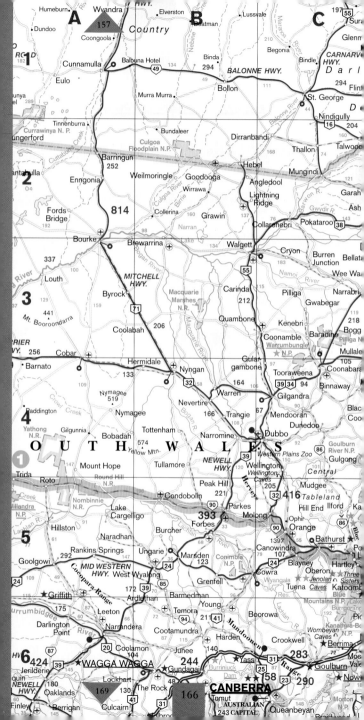

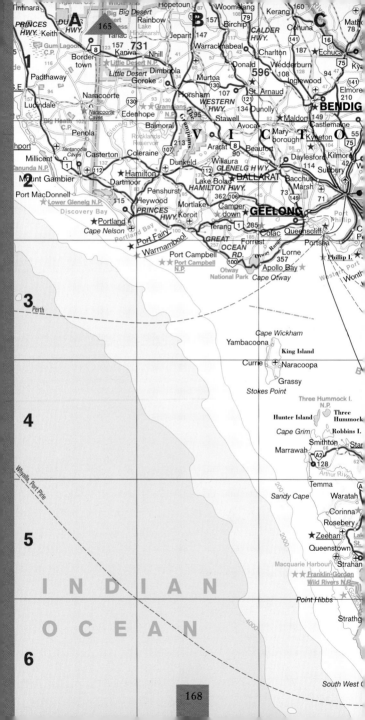

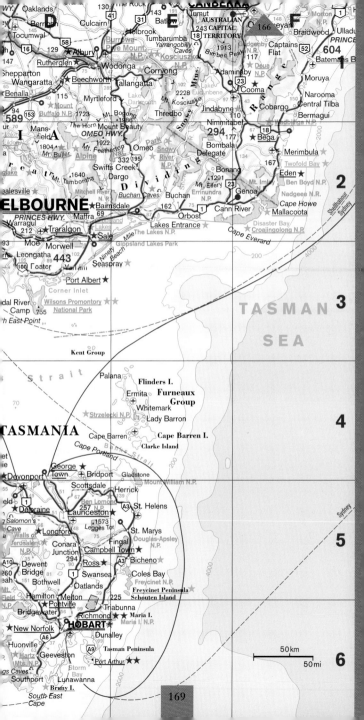

This index lists all the main sights, attractions and museums, National Parks (NP) and Provincial Parks (PP). Numbers in boldface refer to main entries, italics to photographs.

INDEX

What do you get for your money?

 The unit of currency is the Australian dollar A\$, which consists of 100 cents. There are banknotes for 5, 10, 20, 50 and 100 dollars and coins in denominations of 5, 10, 20 and 50 cents and 1 and 2 dollars. The tourist benefits from favourable exchange rates which makes a holiday in the fifth continent an attractive proposition. Recently the Australian dollar has stabilized which means that prices throughout the country have also become stable.

Simple restaurants, pubs, bistros etc. provide good food at moderate prices. In addition, if you are in a hurry, there are many inexpensive fast food outlets and takeaways. Top class restaurants are to be found mainly in the large cities and tourist areas and their prices are correspond-

ingly higher. Also, because of the many immigrants who have come to Australia in recent years, restaurants offering the cuisine of various countries are usually good value.

Flights inside Australia are relativly expensive; a good value alternative is the overland bus service which covers the whole of the country and offers a variety of bus passes. In the cities you get good value for money by purchasing a city tour ticket. Aboriginal carvings and paintings make popular souvenirs. They are slightly cheaper in the country than in the cities where there is more choice, but do look at them carefully to make sure they are genuine. Other places to go looking for bargains are the markets to be found in all cities and large towns throughout the country.

US\$	A\$	£	A\$	Can\$	A\$
1	1.65	1	2.63	1	1.13
2	3.30	2	5.26	2	2.26
3	4.95	3	7.89	3	3.39
4	6.60	4	10.52	4	4.52
5	8.25	5	13.15	5	5.65
10	16.50	10	26.30	10	11.30
15	24.75	15	39.45	15	16.95
20	33.00	20	52.60	20	22.60
25	41.25	25	65.75	25	28.25
30	49.50	30	78.90	30	33.90
40	66.00	40	105.20	40	45.20
50	82.50	50	131.50	50	56.50
60	99.00	60	157.80	60	67.80
70	115.50	70	184.10	70	79.10
80	132.00	80	210.40	80	90.40
90	148.50	90	236.70	90	101.70
100	165.00	100	263.00	100	113.00
200	330.00	200	526.00	200	226.00
300	495.00	300	789.00	300	339.00
400	660.00	400	1052.00	400	452.00
500	825.00	500	1315.00	500	565.00
750	1237.50	750	1972.50	750	847.50
1,000	1650.00	1,000	2630.00	1,000	1130.00